INKED

THE ULTIMATE GUIDE TO POWERFUL CLOSING AND SALES

INKED

NEGOTIATION TACTICS THAT UNLOCK **YES** AND SEAL THE DEAL

JEB BLOUNT

WILEY

Published by John Wiley & Sons, Inc., Hoboken, New Jersey.
Published simultaneously in Canada.

For general information on our other products and services or for technical support, please contact our Customer Care Department within the United States at (800) 762-2974, outside the United States at (317) 572-3993 or fax (317) 572-4002.

Wiley publishes in a variety of print and electronic formats and by print-on-demand. Some material included with standard print versions of this book may not be included in e-books or in print-on-demand. If this book refers to media such as a CD or DVD that is not included in the version you purchased, you may download this material at http://booksupport .wiley.com. For more information about Wiley products, visit www.wiley.com.

Library of Congress Cataloging-in-Publication Data:

Names: Blount, Jeb, author.
Title: Inked : the ultimate guide to powerful closing and sales negotiation
   tactics that unlock yes and seal the deal / Jeb Blount.
Description: Hoboken, New Jersey : Wiley, [2020] | Includes index.
Identifiers: LCCN 2019051504 (print) | LCCN 2019051505 (ebook) | ISBN
   9781119540519 (hardback) | ISBN 9781119540540 (adobe pdf) | ISBN
   9781119540557 (epub)
Subjects: LCSH: Deals. | Negotiation in business.
Classification: LCC HD58.6 .B58 2020 (print) | LCC HD58.6 (ebook) | DDC
   658.85–dc23
LC record available at https://lccn.loc .gov/2019051504
LC ebook record available at https://lccn.loc .gov/2019051505

Printed in the United States of America

F10015928_120319

For Jeb Blount, Jr. I'm so proud of you. Put your sunglasses on son. Your future is very bright!

Contents

Foreword

It's been aptly stated that *all of life is a negotiation,* and nowhere is that more true than in sales! That reality is exactly why it is perplexing that so few of us in sales have ever been properly trained in negotiation.

In this brilliant, necessary, and perfectly titled book, Jeb Blount has provided us *the* ultimate guide on sales negotiation. *INKED* will accomplish more than turning you into a master negotiator; it will deliver on its promise to help you ink many more deals—and you'll close those deals on more favorable terms and at higher margins.

Too many sales teams and individual salespeople are perceived and treated by today's buyers as nothing more than *vendors* or commodity sellers. These sellers neither own their sales process nor set themselves apart as value-creators, and this ineptitude causes them to fall into what I call the "procurement pit," where they're forced to acquiesce to processes and terms dictated by buyers or to sell on price. These ineffective salespeople are unable to differentiate themselves and their solutions and, as a result, also hurt their chance of winning (profitable) business.

I have been a top sales producer for thirty years and have read dozens of sales books, but I gained more keen insights and takeaways about successful negotiating from *INKED* than from all of the others combined and am confident you will, too! That is because the book you are holding (or listening to) was written by today's most in-demand sales trainer specifically for sales professionals.

INKED is real, powerful, and packed with concepts you can implement in your closing call. If you are looking to close more deals, earn higher commissions, crush quota, and qualify for President's Club, then this is the book for you.

The reason Jeb Blount is in such high demand, spends more nights in hotels than anyone I know, and is affectionately known as *the hardest-working man in sales* is that what he teaches works! And one of the main themes running through *INKED* that Jeb wants readers to grasp is that sales negotiation is woven into the sales process, rather than separate from it. Jeb beautifully demonstrates that negotiation isn't a single "thing" or simply a trick or technique. Successful sales negotiation requires mastery of the sales process, the right attitude, planning, tactics, technique, and emotional intelligence.

Prepare to be challenged and entertained. Lower your defense shield, and open your mind. *INKED* lays bare harsh truths. One of the most revealing (and personally convicting) is that effective negotiating begins and ends with emotional discipline and that we sellers hurt our position when we don't rise above the disruptive emotions that emerge during a negotiation. If, like me, your emotional responses often derail your negotiating, you will profusely appreciate Jeb's strong coaching to overcome those emotions and stay focused on the task at hand.

It's never been more imperative for salespeople to raise their negotiating acumen. Today's buyers and procurement professionals are receiving extensive training on "leveling the playing field" and strictly controlling the buying process. The concepts from *INKED* will help you avoid getting commoditized and help you to outsell your competition.

This book is classic Jeb Blount—long on practical advice and examples and short on cheese and gimmicks. Implement the concepts in this book, and you'll become a master sales negotiator. Happy reading (or listening)!

—Mike Weinberg,
author of *New Sales. Simplified*.

PART

I

Introduction to Sales Negotiation

1 | Sales Negotiation as a Discipline

It was a dark night. No stars. Black. Cold. Snow was falling. The only connection we had to the gunman inside the small mobile home was a cell phone. He was holding three hostages and threatening to kill them all.

Earlier in the day he'd lost his temper, and in a fit of rage, shot his wife. As the police arrived, responding to the 911 call, he'd taken her parents and his stepdaughter hostage.

It was another sad case of domestic violence. Every attempt to negotiate a peaceful solution had been stonewalled.

By the time I arrived, things were getting desperate. The gunman had become extremely agitated and fired several rounds at the SWAT team crouched in the snowy woods. He was surrounded with nowhere to go. A violent man with nothing to lose.

Somehow, I had to convince him to back down and let the hostages go. It was a negotiation situation I'd found myself in many times before…

Reality Check

OK, stop! This story is total BS. I'm a sales professional, not a hostage negotiator. No one in their right mind would allow me to get near a situation like this. Don't get me wrong. I negotiate almost every day for a living. But not like this. In the sales profession, it's never life or death (though at times it can feel that way).

Yet this is exactly how so many books on negotiation begin. Their tense narratives include epic boardroom negotiations, dealing with terrorists, negotiating hostage situations, pulling off game-changing mergers, settling massive lawsuits, or mediating international diplomatic crises. Typically, the book's author, portrayed as the hero, pulls off the impossible in the negotiation.

These stories, with all of their drama and tension, make for compelling reading. It's the art of the deal. We love to envision ourselves in those same situations, coolly exerting influence, persuasion, and clever language to turn the tables in our favor and save the day.

But no matter how romantic and compelling the stories, they have absolutely nothing to do with reality in the sales profession. The stories, examples, and techniques discussed in such books are generally focused on:

- Complex, high-stakes negotiations in which each party has many alternatives to a negotiated deal and power plays are the name of the game
- Life or death situations, where neither party can afford to walk away
- Law enforcement and military operations with dire consequences if the negotiation fails

- Governmental, diplomatic, and international relations with the fate of entire countries on the line
- Business mergers and real estate deals
- Legal settlements, including trademarks, intellectual property, and class-action lawsuits
- Resolving conflicts and disagreements, including domestic disputes, personal and business relationship issues, or contract disputes
- Career advancement and salary negotiation
- How to negotiate when *you* are the buyer

There is a massive amount of printed work available on personal, business, diplomatic, legal, and law enforcement negotiation. Some of these books are classics. Many are best sellers. The lessons in these books (and accompanying training programs) are useful.

Except for one problem. These books and training programs fail to address the unique and rapid-fire negotiations that 99% of sales professionals find themselves in each sales day.

Sales Trainers Don't Teach Sales Negotiation

There are few true sales-specific resources on negotiation. A large part of the reason is the false (and perhaps arrogant) belief that sales negotiation is equivalent to all other types of negotiation. That is, the skills, tactics, techniques, patterns, and situations are the same. Sales negotiation, therefore, is lumped in with diplomatic negotiation and attorneys hashing out a class-action lawsuit settlement. But they're not the same.

In addition, there are few true experts and authors who choose to write sales-specific negotiation books. Patrick Tinney's classic *Unlocking Yes: Sales Negotiation Tactics & Strategy* is among the very few exceptions.

Frankly, many sales experts and sales trainers shy away from the subject because they are emotionally uncomfortable with negotiation and find the subject unpalatable. Since many of these same trainers are also poor sales negotiators, salespeople are more likely to encounter contrived BS than training that truly addresses the challenges that they actually face at the sales negotiation table.

Sales Negotiation Is Boring

Adding to all of this is the truth that sales negotiation is boring. There is way more drama when the legal teams from Apple and Qualcomm sit down to work out patent and royalty disputes, or when Chinese and American diplomats negotiate a trade deal. Those negotiations make the front page of the *Wall Street Journal*.

But when…

Maria, an account executive with a SaaS company in San Francisco, is negotiating the per-seat cost of her software with a mid-market company from Waco, Texas;

Joey is working out a deal on a new combine with a farmer in central Pennsylvania;

Jessica is negotiating a lease for 22 commercial trucks with a CEO of a small logistics company located in Des Moines;

Praveen is negotiating an office furniture contract with a large enterprise in New Delhi;

Kendra is negotiating a long-term facility services agreement with a hospital in Singapore;

Colton is negotiating a three-year agreement to put 32 people in rental uniforms at a manufacturing plant in Grand Rapids; or

Robin on my sales team is working out an agreement to train new hires for a payroll processing firm in Dallas

… nobody cares.

Except, of course, for the sales professionals whose compensation depends on the outcome of the negotiations and the companies that depend on those same salespeople to protect their profits.

Millions of sales negotiations take place daily across the globe. Few, if any, ever make the front pages.

Yes, there are exceptions. Certainly, some global account managers are negotiating contract renewals that have far-reaching impact on the enterprise. There are start-ups working on big opportunities that, if won, can generate a flood of venture capital investments. In the overall scheme of things, though, these situations are rare compared to the routine sales negotiations that dominate our profession.

Yet, in these routine and mundane sales negotiations, billions of dollars, rupees, euros, pounds, pesos, yuan, or yen (among other currencies) change hands. The cumulative effect of these mundane sales negotiations directly impacts the profitability, market valuation, customer retention, and long-term viability of the enterprises on whose behalf sales professionals are negotiating.

Author's Note

I use a variety of terms in this book to describe people, companies, and situations.

- **Negotiation Table:** This is the figurative platform for a sales negotiation that may include a physical meeting, telephone or video conversation, email, or text messaging.
- **Stakeholder:** This is an individual person at a prospective or current customer with whom you interact. The stakeholder may play any variety of buying, influence, or negotiation roles.
- **Stakeholder Group:** The array of stakeholders in a deal who are responsible for selecting the vendor of choice.
- **Buyer:** The stakeholder at the table who leads the sales negotiation.
- **Prospect, Account, or Customer:** These terms refer to the enterprise, company, or organization to which the stakeholders belong.

I regularly change terms up to avoid repeating myself and boring my readers. Also note that though many of my examples describe negotiating with new prospects, the techniques described in this book are just as applicable for negotiating with existing accounts.

2 | Salespeople Suck at Negotiating

Before we proceed further, I want to submit into evidence a recent "negotiation" with an account executive who represents one of my vendors. This was all done via email.

Let's begin with some background:

- I've signed several contracts for various services with this vendor, and we have a good working relationship.
- There was no competitor involved, and I had already decided to give the work to the vendor because I trusted them to get it done right.
- I did not have a viable alternative.
- I'd met with the account executive and her team the week before this exchange to outline the project. I gave them a rough budget of $22,000 and asked her to send over an agreement.

On Thursday morning at 10:00 a.m.—one week later: I received an email from the account executive requesting a phone conversation. I responded that I was with a client delivering training and would not be available for a call until the following week. I asked her to send the agreement. She responded with a request for time to meet the next day. Again, I explained that I was with a client and unable to schedule a call until the following week.

This is how the email conversation proceeded:

Account executive opening the negotiation via email (2:54 p.m. Thursday): She responded with an email stating that she and her team had "looked at the requirements of the project and would not be able to do it for less than $35,000." In her words, "Even at this rate, we are barely breaking even."

My response: "I understand, but that's way outside our budget. Please send over the itemized statement of work, and I'll get with my team and see what parts of the project plan we can live without so we can get this inside our budget parameters."

Account executive (5:21 p.m.): "Can we schedule time to talk in the morning at 9:00 a.m. to go over this?"

My response: "No. As I've already explained twice, I'm on premise with one of my clients, delivering a training program, and cannot schedule a call until next week. Please just send over the itemized SOW so we can make some adjustments. I'm sure, with a little effort, we can stay inside our budget for this project and still accomplish our objectives."

Account executive (6:10 p.m.): "I crunched the numbers. Can you possibly go to $32,000? It's our absolute rock bottom."

Me: I did not respond. Instead I went to the gym, grabbed dinner, read a book, and went to bed early.

Account executive (9:00 a.m. on Friday morning): "Jeb, I gave this another look, and I think we can get it down to $29,000. But that's the best we can do and only because you are such a good customer." Note: she still hadn't sent over the itemized SOW I'd requested.

Me: I didn't respond because I was in the classroom delivering training to a group of my client's salespeople and had my phone turned off.

Account executive (12:11 p.m.): "Hey Jeb, just checking in to see if you received my last note that we can do the whole project for only $29K. Should I send over the agreement?"

Me (12:51 p.m.): I glanced at my phone on the way back from lunch and noticed her email. I needed to wrap up training and get to the airport. I marked the account executive's email unread and saved it for later.

Account executive (4:00 p.m. Friday): "Jeb, Good news! The whole team got together and decided that you are such an important customer that we can do the project for $23,000. We love working with you and your team. I know that's a little more than your budget. Will this work?"

Me (4:59 p.m. while in line to board my plane): "That works. Please send over the SOW and contract so we can sign it."

And just like that, the AE had given up $12,000 (a 34% discount from her initial asking price) with no effort on my part. Along the way, she destroyed her credibility.

You may be thinking to yourself, "This is way out there, Jeb— an exception to the rule. This doesn't happen that often."

If you are thinking this, you are wrong. This behavior is common. It happens every day, everywhere. And, sadly, sales negotiation mistakes increase in frequency and are exacerbated at the end of the month, quarter, and year.

I witness my clients' salespeople routinely offering their maximum allowable discount without the stakeholder even asking. Likewise, they are quick to bend on terms and conditions and give away ancillary items without receiving value in exchange. They exhibit no emotional control and no discipline. They perceive that their position is weak, so they often use discounts and price concessions as differentiators.

Every author of every book on negotiating is quick to point out that in business and life, everything is being negotiated and that as humans, we are negotiating naturally at almost every point in our daily lives. But despite this blinding flash of the obvious, despite the fact that salespeople are required to negotiate as part of the job, the brutal and undeniable truth is that most salespeople suck at negotiating.

There are several reasons why salespeople get ripped up like cheap t-shirts by buyers in sales negotiations.

Poor Emotional Discipline

Effective negotiating begins and ends with emotional discipline. When salespeople get beat at the negotiation table—just as in the example above—90% of the time it's due to their inability to rise above disruptive emotions in the moment. Fear, insecurity, anger, attachment, eagerness, desperation, and more all conspire to undermine the salesperson's ability to think clearly and maintain their cool.

Lack of Training

Executives and leaders put tremendous pressure on their sales organizations to hit sales numbers, then complain bitterly after the fact that their salespeople are not negotiating hard enough. The one constant refrain from executives is that their salespeople "leave too much money on the table."

Yet, they invest very little money in training for sales negotiation skills. Nor do they train their sales leaders to model, coach, or reinforce negotiation skills. It's as if salespeople are somehow supposed to be born with the ability to negotiate effectively.

When companies do provide training on negotiation skills, the training content and curriculum is, more often than not, disconnected from the sales process. Sales negotiation is treated as a separate discipline rather than part of an integrated and complete system.

Worse, it's usually delivered by training companies that specialize in teaching negotiation tactics—but *not sales-specific negotiation skills.* Because the trainers that work for these outfits have very little experience selling anything, they are unable to connect the dots between the sales process and the sales negotiation.

In my entire corporate sales and sales leadership career that spanned more than twenty years, I attended only one training session on negotiation. On that occasion, my sales manager used his personal budget to bring in a negotiation training company. In that training, I mostly learned how to negotiate as a buyer which was helpful that year when I was purchasing my first home. Once the training was complete, we called it good and moved on. We never reviewed the material again.

These one-and-done training events feel good but have little long-term impact. Leaders and sales enablement professionals fail to understand that sales negotiation skills are perishable and diminish over time. For this reason, if companies want their salespeople to negotiate at a higher level, there must be a commitment to both initial and ongoing training.

My message to executives: If you want your salespeople to stop leaving money on the table, you must teach them the core competencies, skills, techniques, and emotional intelligence needed to be effective at the *sales* negotiating table. Otherwise, *you* are leaving money on the table.

Failure to Self-Invest

Negotiation is a fundamental part of being a sales professional. No matter who you are and what you sell, you are going to be required to negotiate with buyers.

The companies I worked for didn't provide much in the way of negotiation training, but with my income on the line, I realized that if I didn't become a better negotiator, I was going to pay a price. So, I resolved to invest in myself and get better. I read everything I could get my hands on about negotiation, paid my own way to attend negotiation seminars, and sought out mentors who could help me master negotiation skills, strategies, tactics, and techniques.

In sales, when you out-learn, you out-earn. To become an elite sales athlete, to keep your skills updated and sharp, and to become a master sales negotiator, you must invest your own money, time, and effort in books, audio books, workshops, and online learning programs. You must subscribe to newsletters, podcasts, trade magazines, industry publications, blogs, and sales publications to stay current on your own industry and the sales profession.

Use your drive time wisely. The average inside salesperson has a commute of one to two hours a day. The average outside sales rep spends between four and five hours a day in a car. Turn your car into *automobile university* or your commute into *train, Uber, bus, or plane university.*

Invest that time in learning rather than listening to music or talk radio. Listening to educational and personal development audio programs during your commute or in your car can give you the equivalent of a university education many times over.

Just consider the previous story. How much is this AE losing in commission over the course of a year because she sucks at negotiation? Don't be that account executive.

Buyers Are Better

Buyers, as a rule, generally have more power at the sales negotiating table and are better at negotiating sales outcomes than salespeople. There are several reasons:

- **Training.** Buyers—especially professional buyers who work in procurement—are usually professionally trained in how to negotiate with salespeople and win. Thus, salespeople often find themselves in an amateur versus expert competition. It's like a local club team taking on a professional sports team. The scale is tipped decidedly in the professional's favor.
- **Information and Knowledge.** Buyers typically have more information than the seller. Buyers have entertained presentations and proposals from multiple vendors. They have information on specs, product and service comparisons, and pricing. In general, buyers are doing far more research on competing companies and market conditions than the salespeople they're negotiating with. This information gives them leverage and power when negotiating with less informed sellers.
- **Alternatives.** Buyers tend to have more alternatives than salespeople. This strengthens their power position and lets them exert greater emotional control at the sales negotiation table.

Empty Pipeline ✓ this

The number one reason salespeople are in a weak position and lack emotional discipline at the sales negotiation table is an empty pipeline. When you have an empty pipeline you get desperate. When you get desperate, you get up close and personal with the *Universal Law of Need*.

1. The more you need to close the deal, the more you will give away to close it.
2. The more you need to close the deal, the less likely you are to close it.

Effective prospecting and a full pipeline instantly make salespeople better negotiators. An abundant pipeline gives you emotional control, relaxed, assertive confidence, and the ability to negotiate as if you don't need the deal.

if a client tells me their budget, and I come in higher (slightly) is that stupid?

3 | The Devil Is Discounting: The Case for Improving Sales Negotiation Skills

Sales professionals have been taught to sell value, not price, ad nauseam. I have no doubt that the phrases "sell value" and "demonstrate value" have been drilled into you by leaders and trainers.

Demonstrating value by building a business case for how you and your company will deliver measurable business outcomes is crucial for both competitive differentiation and improving your power position at the sales negotiation table.

Along with demonstrating value, helping stakeholders look beyond price to the *total cost of ownership* (TCO) makes it easier to build apples to apples comparisons in competitive situations.

Still, if we are keeping it real, price matters. It is the ticket into the game. As much as sales trainers are wont to downplay the role that price plays, the sales professionals who are working in the trenches know it matters.

- Price is what buyers will fixate on.
- Price, and the terms and conditions attached to the price, will likely determine how your commission or bonus is calculated for the sale.
- Price, and the terms and conditions attached to the price, directly impacts your company's profit margin.
- Price is what you will negotiate and agree on before doing business.
- Price is what you are most likely to discount in order to close the deal.

And you will discount. In the real world, you will need to make concessions to get deals done. The problem is that most salespeople are giving away far more in discounts than is required to win deals because, as we've established, they suck at negotiating.

The Path of Least Resistance to a Commission Check

Salespeople have a bad tendency of taking the path of least re-sistance to a commission check. In doing so, they leave a massive amount of money on the table for themselves and their employers.

I get it because I've been there, done that, and have the tattoo and t-shirt to prove it. You really want the deal, are desperate to put a number on the board, or maybe just dig the rush of getting ink. It feels easier and safer in the moment to give it all away and get the deal instead of taking the risk that you'll negotiate and get nothing.

Early in my career, my sales manager called me into his office. On his desk was a spreadsheet that told the story of a curious pattern in my deal-making. He pointed out that I became a much better negotiator once I'd wrapped up quota.

It was January, at the beginning of a new sales year. He walked me through my average discounts from our book rates before and after I made quota the previous year.

Before the third week in September, my average discount from book was 22.7%, which was all of the 20% leeway my company allowed me to reduce prices without management approval, plus the additional discounts I'd convinced my leadership team to approve in order to close many of my bigger deals.

The shocker was what happened to my discounts after I had made my number for the year. He showed me that after I'd made quota, my discounts had dropped to just 9%, *and* the average number of deals I'd inked per month had actually gone up.

As soon as I saw the evidence in black and white, I knew the truth. Once I didn't *need* to win, I approached stakeholders differently. I started closing assumptively and *asking* for exactly what I wanted.

Stakeholders bent to my will. I sold new accounts at higher prices. I confidently asked for full fees and payment for ancillary items that we would usually write off to get the deal. I secured longer contractual commitments along with more favorable terms and conditions.

Before making my number, I was afraid that if I didn't give big discounts, I'd lose sales to my competitors. The data proved that my closing ratio did just the opposite. Even though I stopped handing out big discounts like candy, it went up. I closed account after account at higher prices, and my commissions grew bigger because the commission plan richly rewarded high-profit deals.

It was these observations of my own behavior that began my fascination with sales negotiation. I began to study, hone, and master sales negotiation tactics that reduced the need for discounting. As my income grew, I had more money to save and invest. I was able to max out my 401(k) plan and buy a home rather than rent. I bought a few fun "toys" for the driveway as well. When I looked around, I was making far more than my peers and my friends.

This epiphany happened in my twenties. Today, through the magic of compound interest, the extra money I put away from my larger commission checks has grown exponentially. Those investments gave me financial freedom, allowed me to start my company, Sales Gravy, and will take care of my family in retirement.

When you discount, you aren't just reducing your income today; you are also impacting your savings and future income. There are dozens of calculators on the internet that will show you the future value of the money that you earn and save today.

For example, let's say that through improved negotiation, you conservatively add an additional $10,000 to your income this year and invest that money. In thirty years, that $10K at a modest 5% return rate will be worth $44,677. That's a lot of dough, and it is absolutely within your grasp. You just need to master sales negotiation skills.

Cost of Discounting Exercise #1

1. Make a list of every deal you've sold over the past twelve months.
2. Next, calculate the total discount on each of those sales (as a percentage) from your standard pricing.
3. Add all the discounts together and divide by the total number of deals sold. This is your average discount percentage.
4. Now calculate your total commissions, spiffs, and bonuses on those sales.
5. Finally, get out your calculator and commission plan. Do the math. Figure out how much more you would have earned had you reduced your average discount percentage by just 5%, 10%, 15%, 20%, and so on.

Ode to the Maximum Discount

Salespeople have a terrible habit of giving away their maximum discount rather than holding on to their leverage. If they have the leeway to give 20% off the price to close the deal, that's where they begin. Whether their decision is conscious or subconscious, they do everything possible to avoid negotiating, get a quick yes, close the deal, and move on to the next one.

In line with this bad habit is discounting in large increments: 5%, 10%, and 20% at a time.

Recently, while working with an inside sales team in San Francisco, I observed this behavior. The average opening discount was 10%. This was where almost every rep started on every negotiation, every time. Subsequent moves were in 10% increments.

The reps had the leeway to discount up to 30% before getting a manager's approval for more. The average discount across all the new deals was right at 25%.

Our objective with this client was to reduce the average discount from 25% to 20% (a modest five percent) without reducing the number of new accounts sold or changing the negotiating limit of the sales professionals. Working with the sales leadership team, we set three new rules for discounting:

Lower the opening discount: The opening discount could be no greater than 5%. The sales reps were stunned at how many prospects said yes to this much lower opening move.

Pattern disruption: We moved to unpredictable increments. Rather than a discounting rhythm of 5%, then 5% more, and then another 5%, we shifted to 4.7%, then 3.1% more, and then another 2.4%. This disrupted the discounting pattern that buyers expected and required them to engage in the process. In addition, lowering the discount percentage on each move signaled that the floor was approaching. ⟵ floor

Leverage precise numbers: The human brain considers precise numbers like 4.7% or $47 more legitimate than 5% or $50.

Therefore, there is a higher probability that the buyer will quickly agree to accept a more precise concession, but they will continue to negotiate when the concession is an even number.

At the end of the first week, with the salespeople operating under these new rules, the average discount on the closed-won deals dropped from 25% to 17%. But what shocked everyone was that the number of deals closed increased!

When the leadership team did the math, the 8% reduction in discounts, over the course of a year, added up to over $30 million in new sales revenue—without adding headcount or spending a dime on marketing and lead generation.

When they extrapolated this out over the lifetime value of the monthly recurring revenue (MRR) of the new customers, taking into account the average churn and account expansion, the number crossed $200 million. It all added up to increased market valuation, profits that could be invested back into growth initiatives, and a brilliant story to tell their investors.

Cost of Discounting Exercise #2

If you are a leader, executive, or business owner, take a moment to analyze what a reduction in discounting would look like for your entire sales team. Do the following:

1. Make a list of every deal your salespeople have sold over the past twelve months.
2. Next, calculate the total discount from your standard pricing on each of those sales.
3. Add all the discounts together and divide by the total number of deals closed. This is the average discount for your sales team.
4. Do the math. Calculate the additional sales revenue and associated profit your organization would have driven to the top line and dropped through to the bottom line had you

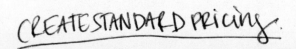

CREATE STANDARD PRICING.

> reduced your average discount percentage by 5%, 10%, 15%, 20%, and so on.
> 5. Finally, calculate the lifetime value of those reduced discounts for your new accounts.

For most companies, like my client in the story above, the numbers are shocking. And it's not just discounting. For one of the companies we advise, teaching their salespeople to negotiate to get payment within twenty-four hours versus giving customers five days to pay once the deal was inked instantly dropped an additional $1.7 million in profit to the bottom line.

I recommend sitting down with your leadership and finance team and running through this exercise in great detail. Consider how the additional new sales revenue and profits would change your organization and how you can help each salesperson see how much it is costing them personally to leave so much money on the table.

Then work together to set clear goals and reasonable targets for reducing discounts with more effective sales negotiating strategies and tactics. Be careful, though, not to become so draconian that you reduce the number of deals you are closing as an unintended consequence. Remember, it's a balance.

The easiest, fastest way to accelerate revenue growth while dropping more to the bottom line, without making large investments in sales headcount and capital projects or increasing advertising and marketing expenses, is to simply reduce discounting. And the fastest path to reducing discounting is teaching your salespeople, account managers, and customer success team to become better sales negotiators.

4 | Sales Negotiation Skills Are Not One-Size-Fits-All

My objective with this book is to give you a playbook and field guide for becoming a more effective sales negotiator. Although this book is primarily focused on business-to-business (B2B) sales negotiation, the concepts may easily be applied to business-to-consumer (B2C) sales situations.

However, there are few one-size-fits-all solutions in sales, and negotiation is no exception. In the sales profession, context matters. There is little black and white.

I will not be able to provide explicit instructions for handling every conceivable sales negotiation situation. For you, some things I teach in this book may not apply. It is important that we acknowledge this as we begin our journey together.

- Negotiation complexity shifts with the situation. Enterprise-level and long-cycle complex sales negotiation is much different from transactional, one-call-close haggling.
- Negotiating with a stakeholder who *works for* a business is different from negotiating directly with a business *owner.*
- Negotiating with C-level and senior executives is far different from working out a deal with a middle manager.
- Negotiating with procurement is vastly different from negotiating with an engaged stakeholder.
- B2B negotiation is different from negotiating with individual consumers in B2C sales.
- Negotiating over physical products is different from negotiating for intangible services and software.

However, as a sales professional, you are going to be required to negotiate no matter your unique situation. So keep an open mind and judge for yourself which ideas, strategies, techniques, and tactics apply and will work best in your unique situation.

The Seven Rules of Sales Negotiation

There are, however, *seven rules of sales negotiation* common to all sales situations that will guide you on your journey to mastering sales negotiation skills. These rules are the foundation for the lessons in this book.

What I will promise is that when you internalize these rules and play by them, you will become a more effective negotiator, you will bring home more profitable accounts for your company, and your income will grow.

Win First, Then Negotiate

This is *rule one* in sales negotiation. It's also the rule that most salespeople consistently violate. Getting the timing wrong with negotiation causes you to give your leverage away early and for free. Do not negotiate until your stakeholders have named you the vendor of choice (VOC)—either explicitly or implicitly.

Before that point, you are not negotiating. You may be dealing with price objections, bidding against your competitors, using price concessions as a differentiation tool, or negotiating with yourself, but you are not in a sales negotiation with the buyer.

Play to Win

Forget about "win–win" outcomes and start playing to win. Your job as a sales professional is to win for your team. To become an effective sales negotiator, you must gain a clear picture of the negotiation chess board before you enter the game and get comfortable with winning for your team.

Protect Relationships

In all but the most transactional deals, the relationship matters. You cannot use hard-nosed tactics and cheesy negotiation gambits if you want to retain your customers over the long term. Therefore, you must win for your team *and* protect your relationships with stakeholders. These two endeavors are not mutually exclusive. This requires mastering Sales EQ and *dual process communication*—a focus on empathy and outcome.

Emotional Discipline Wins

At the sales negotiation table, the person who exerts the greatest amount of emotional control has the highest probability of getting the outcome they desire. Mastering sales negotiation begins and ends with mastering your own disruptive emotions.

To Master Sales Negotiation, You Must Master the Sales Process

The real secret to mastering sales negotiation is mastering the sales process. There is no negotiation technique, no move, no play, no gambit that will save you from a failure to follow and execute the sales process.

Being an effective closer, making the case for change, gathering the ammunition you need to minimize objections, and gaining the leverage to negotiate effectively and win for your team require excellence throughout the entire sales process—step, by step, by step, by step.

Never Give Leverage Away for Free

When you have something someone else wants, you have leverage. You may use leverage to compel people to change their behavior, change the shape of time, move toward your position, and make concessions. For this reason, leverage is currency, and it must be used as such. It has value and must be exchanged for value. Effective sales negotiators never give away leverage without getting something of equal or greater value in return.

Eliminate and Neutralize Alternatives

Buyers derive power at the sales negotiation table through alternatives to negotiating an outcome with you. The more alternatives they have, the stronger their power position and the weaker yours. Therefore, your overriding focus throughout the sales process journey must be on improving your power position and win probability by eliminating or neutralizing the buyer's perceived alternatives to doing business with you.

Hold the Cheese

If you are familiar with my work, you know that I eschew contrived and cheesy tactics that never work in the real world and only serve to destroy your credibility. I focus on the basics and fundamentals—even when those fundamentals are not bright, shiny, new, or sexy.

My mission is to help you become a better negotiator so that you make more money. Pandering to you will not get that job done. The brutal fact is that no magic pill or easy button will make you a master negotiator. There isn't a killer chess move that will give you the power to ink the deal on your terms every time.

Positive negotiated outcomes depend heavily on your ability to navigate and manage the sales process effectively. The basics and fundamentals of prospecting, executing the sales process, emotional control, interpersonal skills, and human influence are always in play.

Sales negotiation is often rapid, in the moment, and conducted via multiple communication channels. It's not unusual to find yourself negotiating by phone, email, text, direct message, video calls, web chat, as well as in person.

It's rare that there is a formal negotiating meeting set in advance that gives all parties time to prepare and strategize. You won't be setting the stage, arranging the room just so, or spending months with your team in a war room building a complex strategic plan.

Sales negotiation is woven into the sales process rather than separate from it. This certainly doesn't mean that you won't have meetings set specifically for closing and negotiating. Some buyers will want to carefully consider your proposal and then meet with you to negotiate and ink the deal.

These days, though, you are more likely to be negotiating on a short impromptu phone call or via email than sitting in a conference room, going back and forth with buyers. The sales negotiation "table," like so many other things, has moved to the cloud.

In this environment, you must be adaptable, flexible, and agile, and prepared to negotiate at any time, in any place, and through any channel.

Free Sales Negotiation Training Resources

I've compiled a large collection of free resources to help you become a master negotiator and achieve excellence throughout the sales process. This twelve-month membership package, valued at $1,200, is yours free with this book purchase.

Just go to https://www.fanaticalprospecting.com, choose the Professional Level Membership, then use CODE: *INKED724* at checkout. No credit card or payment of any kind is required to access these free resources.

PART

II

On Winning

5

Sales Negotiation Is About Winning for Your Team

People, especially salespeople and those who manage them, often use the phrase "win-win" and negotiation in the same breath. The concept of negotiating win-win outcomes certainly makes sense in diplomacy, arbitration, and conflict resolution.

"Win-win" is a noble concept. It's nice when everyone wins. If both sides can walk away winners that's a good thing. But win-win should not be your primary objective at the sales negotiation table, because as a sales professional, your objective is to win for *your* team.

Salespeople delude themselves into believing that everyone needs to win and that negotiated outcomes must be "fair and equitable." "Win-win" makes sense. Fair and equitable is an easy concept to wrap your mind and emotions around. Yet, it's just another verse of "Sales Kumbaya."

For far too many salespeople, the fixation on "win–win" is an excuse for avoiding the uncomfortable and natural conflict inherent in negotiation. It's a cop-out—an easy way to justify why you just gave the other side your maximum discount without a fight.

Here's a brutal truth that you need to internalize: "Win–win" is the warm blanket of delusion where your commission check and your company's profits curl up to die. "Win–win" as an outcome goal in sales negotiation is total BS. If you are focused on "win–win," there is a real good chance that you are losing. Sales negotiation is about getting the best possible outcome for your team. Period.

Salespeople who lead with a "win–win" mindset get destroyed at the sales negotiation table because (trust me on this) your buyer isn't negotiating with you for a "win–win" outcome. They are negotiating *to win for their team*. Savvy buyers know exactly how to leverage the *win-win-fair-and-equitable* mindset to move salespeople from positions of strength to positions of weakness and then pick their pockets.

When salespeople engage in sales negotiations with a focus on "win–win," the most likely outcome is that they allow their eagerness to make their buyer happy—falsely equating a happy buyer with winning—and to override reason and give away the farm.

Relationships Matter

Yet, sales negotiation is woven into the fabric of the long-term relationships you have either built or hope to build with your customer's stakeholder group. Except in purely transactional sales, in which the long-term relationship is unimportant, you don't negotiate to win in a vacuum.

In sales negotiations, you cannot lose sight of the lifetime value of the relationships you've developed and nurtured. In other words, relationships matter and must be protected.

Your job is to win for your team. But even when your negotiating position is strong and you have the leverage to extract maximum flesh, winning at the expense of your buyer or causing them to lose face can create resentment that will cost you dearly down the road. Winning for the sake of winning is a poor long-term strategy.

Therefore, sales negotiation is often a paradox—a *dual process* of empathy *and* outcome; you must win for your team *and* protect your relationships.

Mitigate Resentment

Resentment is a monster that degrades and destroys relationships. Resentment can go both ways. When stakeholders feel that you took advantage of their weak position or lack of information, it may seriously impact the future of your relationship. On the other hand, when you give too much away and feel resentment at being used or taken advantage of, it can negatively impact how you and your team value, serve, and interact with your customer.

I've been there and have the scars to prove it. I've negotiated poorly from a position of weakness and ended up hating my customer for it. The contempt I felt for them eventually caused the business relationship to unravel. It was not my customer's fault (they were winning for their team). It was mine for allowing it to happen and not considering the unintended consequences of inking a bad deal.

Some buyers get this. They are good partners who understand the negative impact that resentment and the resulting feeling of contempt have on relationships. These buyers are good partners. They focus on negotiating the best deal for their company while remembering that you must make a profit in order to give them the service and customer experience they expect.

Far more often though, buyers are either too myopic to understand this concept or simply don't care. This is almost always true when you are dealing with procurement.

Procurement (sometimes called purchasing or contracting) has a singular mission: to extract the best terms for their organization and squeeze the maximum discount out of you. They don't care if you make money or if the negotiated terms and conditions handcuff you and make it difficult to serve them. When the dust clears, they won't be dealing with you. They'll hand you back to the account stakeholders and wash their hands of it all.

But it is not the buyer's job to think ahead to the unintended consequences of a lopsided deal and the resentment that it might cause for either party. It is *your* responsibility to think long-term and consider the lifetime value of the customer. There are times when:

- You'll need to be the adult in the room. You must rationally and logically consider the best interests of both parties. You must be willing to make the right decisions and, at times, sacrifice a short-term win for a long-term profitable partnership.
- The buyer's jugular is exposed, and you can easily go in for the kill, but you need to pull back, play the long game, and allow them to save face in the moment.
- You need to transparently and honestly explain to the other side the negative impact on service delivery and customer experience when all of the profit is drained from the deal or the terms and conditions of the agreement are not aligned with reality.
- You'll need to walk away from a bad deal. Rather than risking the long-term relationship with your stakeholders (and your reputation), let your competitor crash and burn on the bad deal so that you can live to fight another day.

Once, my team and I were working on a monster deal with a large regional grocery store chain. This company had the reputation for being a premium brand. Its stores were pristine, and its customer demographic was upper-income professionals.

We'd been working diligently and methodically on the opportunity for two years. Finally, the stakeholder group named us the vendor of choice (VOC). At that point, we were sent to their procurement team to work out the details of a five-year multimillion-dollar contract for weekly service delivery to more than 200 locations. We celebrated!

The stakeholder group selected my company because we had committed to a quality control and service delivery process that aligned with their value system and mission. Our proposal had a higher unit price than our competitors, but we had successfully demonstrated that our total cost of ownership (TCO) would be lower over the course of the contract.

At the negotiation table, though, it didn't seem to matter. Because of their size, the company had massive buying power and leverage. The procurement team was accustomed to leveraging that power like a sledgehammer. Vendors that wanted to do business with them quickly capitulated.

We were immediately bludgeoned with the significantly lower unit prices that our competitors had proposed. These low prices, by the way, did not provide the margins required to deliver on the service and quality expectations of the stakeholder group. Along with beating us up over our pricing, procurement introduced stringent one-sided terms and conditions that penalized us heavily for even small issues—with little recourse if the issue proved to be their fault, not ours.

We were torn. All we had to do was agree to their terms. We would land a huge account and get an immediate injection of top-line revenue that we sorely needed. Our group had been underperforming the rest of the company, and there was intense pressure to turn things around. Yet, agreeing to those terms would make it difficult to squeeze out a profit or deliver on their high expectations.

We'd worked so long and so hard for the deal, and we wanted it badly. In the end, though, we walked away. It was our best alternative.

It was also gut-wrenching and absolutely heartbreaking. I'll never forget that feeling. The other side was unmovable in their demands, and we were unable to get them to make any concessions. They awarded the contract to the competitor that came in with the lowest price.

Eighteen months later, my phone rang. The head of their store operations was on the other line. He explained that our competitor was failing to deliver on all fronts, so they needed to make a move. He was curious if we'd be interested in reengaging.

Shortly afterwards, we negotiated a contract on much better terms. That was seventeen years ago. Though I am no longer with that company, they still service the grocery store chain, and the relationship is stronger than ever.

Satisfaction and Contentment

Think for a moment about what people are really negotiating for. It's not money, terms, conditions, savings, risk reduction, ROI, measurable business outcomes, or any of the logical things we typically believe are on the table. Don't get me wrong. Those things are very important, but it's just not what people are negotiating for.

People negotiate first and foremost for satisfaction and contentment. They want to:

- Feel significant and important
- Feel that they are good negotiators
- Feel self-worth for doing a good job
- Please their boss
- Feel the satisfaction of winning
- Feel that they have won for their team
- Save face and protect their self-esteem

By the way, you want the same things. Even the "robots" in procurement, who have no emotional connection to you or what they are buying, want to feel that they have done worthwhile work by squeezing you for concessions. They want satisfaction.

What we know to be true, because neuroscience has proven[1] that it's true, is that sales negotiation begins and ends with emotion. Emotion comes first, then logic.

This is exactly why, in every sales negotiation, the person who exerts the greatest emotional discipline has the highest probability of getting the outcome they desire. (This theme and these words will be repeated again and again in the pages of this book.)

Therefore, we cannot separate emotions from negotiation. Instead we must be aware of the role emotions play in the heat of the moment and how they affect both short- and long-term outcomes. We must master techniques for managing our own disruptive emotions so that we may rise above them and influence the emotions and behaviors of other people.

We'll take a deeper dive into emotional discipline in an upcoming chapter. First, let's get back to resentment.

Resentment and Contempt

What's the opposite of satisfaction and contentment? It's resentment. And resentment breeds contempt.

Resentment and contempt are the gangrene of relationships, festering below the surface, often unspoken, slowly rotting away the connections that bind people together until the relationship is destroyed.

> **Resentment** is defined as bitterness, indignation, irritation, displeasure, dissatisfaction, disgruntlement, discontentment, discontent, resentfulness, bad feelings, hard feelings, ill feelings, acrimony, rancor, animosity, hostility, jaundice, antipathy, antagonism, enmity, and hate.[2] (That's a mouthful of negativity.)
>
> **Contempt** is defined as the feeling with which a person regards anything considered mean, vile, or worthless; disdain and scorn.[3] It's a lack of respect accompanied by a feeling of intense dislike.[4]

These are the two most powerful negative emotions in the pantheon of human emotions.

Resentment is a multilayered, complex emotion that is most often replayed and relived over and over in our minds—thus leading to the emotion of contempt. It's triggered most often from an insult or an emotional injury like rejection, humiliation, losing face (especially in front of other people), a perceived injustice, feeling used or taken advantage of, embarrassment, feeling that you've been belittled, or being diminished—especially when your social status and importance are attacked.

Resentment can be so emotionally debilitating that it is impossible to deal rationally with someone who is in this state and consumed by the emotion. It triggers anger and hatred, potentially leading to emotional blow-ups. Worse, it generates feelings of cynicism, paranoia, and distrust. It can morph into a confirmation bias, causing the resentful person to perceive every action of the target of their resentment to be negatively aimed at them.

Sales negotiation is not about creating "win-win" outcomes. Instead, it is about winning for your team. But at the same time, it is a dual process in which you must balance preserving the relationship with winning. This requires awareness, empathy, and tact.

At the sales negotiation table, you must never lose sight of the long-term consequences of the negotiated outcome. Sometimes you'll need to stand up and be the adult in the room in order to mitigate future resentment on both sides of the table.

This is why it is critically important that you and your team understand how and why resentment is created at the sales negotiation table. Once it is triggered, communication and cooperation are often severed, creating a downward spiral that is not easily reversed. In this untenable situation, marred by distrust and lack of transparency, it becomes impossible to save the relationship.

6 | Sales Negotiation Rule One: Win First, Then Negotiate

The first and most important rule of sales negotiation is: *win first and then negotiate.* In other words, avoid negotiating price, terms, and conditions until the buyer or stakeholder group has selected you as their vendor of choice (VOC).

Until that point, you are not negotiating. You may be dealing with objections, waging a bidding war with your competitors, giving away all of your leverage for free, or making one-sided concessions as you negotiate with yourself. But you are *not* negotiating.

Negotiation begins *after* the sales process ends and begins when the buyer or stakeholder group has selected you as the VOC.

Once the stakeholders have chosen you, it dramatically changes their motivation curve. It brings down emotional walls and turns the opaque transparent. It makes it easier to gain consensus on a deal. Most importantly, stakeholders are much more likely to see the deal through to an outcome—reducing the probability that it stalls in your pipeline.

Winning first makes it easier for you to maintain emotional control, exude relaxed yet assertive confidence, get what you want, and close the sale.

Rope-a-Dope

Jason presented his proposal for the contract renewal to the vice president of operations and her team on a Monday morning. He'd been the account manager for this customer for the past four years.

It was a key account and losing it to a competitor would be devastating to his commission check and his region. There was a lot at risk.

Jason had bent over backwards to take care of the account and had data demonstrating the value that his company had delivered. He'd been named the supplier of the year twice. Inside the account, his relationships were deep and wide, however he also knew that this account was a big target for his competitors and that they would work hard to displace him.

Following his final presentation, the vice president said, "Jason, thank you for your proposal. It was well thought out. You and your company have done a nice job for us over the years. But we are under pressure to lower our costs going into the new fiscal year. That's why we've entertained quotes from your competitors. Based on what they've brought us, I'm going to need you to sharpen your pencil on this proposal."

"So, this means that you are planning to renew your contract with us and we just need to work on some numbers?" Jason asked confidently.

"We haven't made that decision yet. We plan to award the contract on Friday. Because you've done such a good job, we're giving you a chance to come back with better pricing," said the VP, pointing to the pricing page on his proposal.

Jason remained firm, "I appreciate that. I stand by our pricing, though. It is competitive and will ensure that we can continue to provide the service levels you expect."

With that, the meeting ended. As Jason pulled into the parking lot back at his office, he was feeling nervous. But he knew that his prices were consistent with the market, that his customer would incur considerable cost and pain in changing vendors. He had advocates inside the account that were on his side and would fight for him.

On Wednesday morning he received a call from the VP: "Jason, we are making a decision about the contract on Friday. As a friend, I want to give you one more chance to sharpen your pencil on this."

Jason politely repeated that he felt his proposal was fair.

On Friday morning his phone rang again. It was the VP again, The VP was back on the line "Jason, we're going over all the proposals this morning before we make our final decision. I want to give you one last chance to take a second look at your numbers. Just between you and me, I highly recommend that you do."

Jason politely declined and took a moment to reiterate the value of and the case for continuing the relationship.

At one o'clock, the VP was back on the line, awarding him the contract. Jason thanked her and said he looked forward to extending the relationship. He was also curious and asked why he'd been selected over his competitors that had offered lower prices.

"All of your competitors except one came in with roughly the same pricing as your proposal. There was one competitor that came in significantly lower than you, but we didn't feel we could trust them to deliver on their promises. There really wasn't a compelling enough reason to give any of them a second look. I was just testing you to see if you'd give us a price concession."

This story is true. Savvy buyers play such games every day to provoke fear in salespeople and gain price discounts. For most salespeople, though, it doesn't play out this way. They are unable to maintain emotional discipline and stick to their guns. Under pressure, they negotiate with themselves and make concessions. It's classic rope-a-dope, a boxing strategy credited to Muhammed Ali in which he allowed his opponents to burn all of their energy swinging at air.

Buyers use many different types of rope-a-dope tactics to pull you in and wear you out emotionally before you even get to the negotiating table. By pushing you to negotiate with yourself, the buyer drains you of both your leverage and energy before the sales negotiation even begins. When you are in this weakened state, they easily swoop in for the kill and get a win for their team.

But How Do I Know I've Won?

When I lead Sales Negotiation Skills training and teach sales professionals to win first and then negotiate, I get hit with this question:

> This doesn't make sense. How can I possibly know that I've won? I mean, if I've won, isn't the negotiation already over?

The primary reason why the concept "win first, then negotiate" confounds salespeople is that they've never been in this position. They have no idea what it feels like to be selected as the VOC before negotiating. Instead, they are:

1. Showing up and throwing up.
2. Pitch-slapping buyers with features and benefits rather than asking questions and doing discovery.
3. Skipping steps in the sales process.
4. Ceding control of the sales conversation and process to the buyer.
5. Presenting generic marketing drivel rather than tailored solutions and measurable business outcomes.

Because they fail at practically every phase of the sales process, they are battling price from the first conversation. It's not uncommon to find these salespeople lowering their price in the first few minutes of the initial meeting with a stakeholder. Since they bring nothing unique to the table, the only place to differentiate is price. And that's where buyers hammer them.

Sadly, these salespeople think this is negotiating. But they are not negotiating with the buyer; they are negotiating with themselves.

This leaves them caught between a rock and a hard place—buyers who demand price concessions and their leaders who tell them they need to negotiate harder. The result is diminished confidence, miserable one-sided conversations with stakeholders, lost income, and lower self-esteem.

My Favorite Words

I've always said that my favorite words to hear from a buyer's lips after I've presented my final proposal are, *"Jeb, we really want to do business with you, but ..."* I love these words because they mean I've won. I'm the vendor of choice. I'm the person they trust most to solve their problems and help them achieve their desired business outcomes.

It means that they've bought me. I've done my job in the sales process, and all we must do now is negotiate the *but*. We must bridge the *value gap*—the space between how the stakeholders and I each value my business case and proposal.

The term *proposal* is important. I don't and never will negotiate until a formal proposal has been delivered. Until that point, I may be dealing with hard questions and objections, or the stakeholder may even ask me to make a price concession in order to start the sales process, but until I am selected, I hold the line. I am not negotiating.

A proposal is essentially a written offer to buy—that offer may be a presentation, quote, formal proposal, RFP response, or a contract that you present. In simple transactional sales, it may be a verbal offer or the published list price.

There cannot be a negotiation on the price, terms, or conditions until an offer is made. Before that point, you may acquiesce and make concessions, but when you do so you are negotiating with yourself, which strengthens the other side's position and weakens yours.

Explicit Choice

In some cases, your stakeholder will tell you outright that they want to do business with you.

This can be a verbal commitment that clearly indicates that you are their primary choice like, "We really want to do business with you."

In other cases, especially in complex deals that go through an RFP or tender, your prospect may provisionally award you the contract with the caveat that you'll need to negotiate specific items and go through their contracting process.

Implicit Choice

In other situations, there is an implicit choice. This requires you to pay attention to your intuition and apply deep listening. You'll be paying attention to how they interact with you, how open and transparent they are when answering questions, how they speak about your competitors, and how effective you are at aligning their buying process with your sales process.

In larger deals in which you have a coach or executive sponsor, you may get informal word that the stakeholder group has selected you. In most cases, this is how I know that I've won.

When looking for implicit clues that you've won, pay close attention to five stakeholder behaviors:

- The stakeholder group's emotional engagement, their willingness to match your effort, and a consistent willingness to make and keep micro-commitments of time and action
- Positive signals from executive sponsors and coaches, like a "whisper in your ear" that you've won
- When it is clear that the other competitors have been eliminated
- When there doesn't appear to be another viable alternative
- Commitment to future implementation, installation, transition, migration, or delivery dates

When you feel that an implicit choice has been made, before you negotiate, stop and close for an explicit selection.

Stakeholder: "This is looking good. We like your platform. However, the seat price is a little higher than we have in our budget. We need to get it to $50 per seat for it to work for us. Your competitors are much lower. What can you do?"

Sales professional (closing): "OK. Let me ask you a question. If I'm able to make that happen for you, can we get the agreement approved and signed today?"

Stakeholder: "Yes. We are ready to move forward with you."

Sales professional: "Great. Let me see what I can do. May we schedule a call for two o'clock to regroup?"

Notice that the sales professional used her leverage—a potentially lower per-seat price for the SaaS platform—to get the stakeholder to explicitly select her company. Yet she gave nothing away and made no commitment, other than to work toward the stakeholder's budgetary requirement. She also gained a commitment for a formal meeting to negotiate and ink the final deal, giving herself time to plan her approach.

The first step toward mastering sales negotiation is internalizing rule one: *win* first, *then* negotiate.

7

Timing Matters: Avoid Negotiating Red Herrings and Objections

A big problem for salespeople is that they tend to chase negotiation red herrings early in the sales process, causing them to give their leverage away for free and handcuff themselves with one-sided early concessions.

A red herring is something that distracts you from your focus, misleads you, or diverts your attention from the objective of your sales conversation. For example, during your initial meeting, before any discovery has been done, the stakeholder tells you that they've been doing research online and seen that your competitor's prices are much lower. They want to know if you'll match them.

It's so easy to get drawn into defending your pricing in situations like this and lose control of the conversation and your leverage. This is why you must avoid getting distracted by red herrings at all costs.

The term *red herring* is thought to originate from the practice of dragging a dead fish across a trail to pull hounds off the scent. And this is exactly what happens when you abandon the objective of your call to chase a red herring. Rather than controlling the agenda, moving toward your targeted next step, advancing the sale, and preserving your leverage, you start negotiating with yourself.

Without thinking, you lose emotional control and give away terms, conditions, and discounts. Or you: make special promises before you've fully qualified the opportunity; engaged your prospect in discovery; gained insight into their values, problems, opportunities, desired outcomes, and metrics that matter; and built the case to be their vendor of choice.

Red herring negotiations are most likely to occur on initial meetings, at the start of demos and presentations, and at presentations to a group of stakeholders. Red herrings often seem innocuous—just simple statements or questions:

- "Look, before we go any further, I need to know that you aren't too expensive."
- "Your competitor quoted us this price. Can you match that?"
- "You need to know that we don't want to sign a long-term contract."
- "Your competitor promised they could do _____. Can you do that too?"
- "This is all of the budget we have for this project. Can you work with that?"
- "We are already in discussions with your competitor, and they're offering up some nice incentives. Tell us what you can do for us that they can't."

Do not take the bait! Red herrings, if you manage them poorly, are emotional hijackers that destroy your ability to negotiate effectively. When you chase red herrings, you:

- Give away your leverage without getting anything in return
- Show your hand to the stakeholder and potentially your competitors
- Skip the sales process
- Weaken your power position
- Cede control to your stakeholder and become their puppet

When you are faced with a red herring in a negotiation, the key is emotional control. Even though your brain might delude you into believing that you can shortcut the sales process and close the sale with a quick negotiation, do not give in to that feeling. Even though you feel an obligation to answer the question and are eager to do that and please the buyer, don't do it.

Stick to the sales process. It is the sales process that allows you to build a business case that strengthens your power position and gives you leverage at the negotiation table.

PAIS

When you get thrown a red herring during a negotiation, you must manage your emotions and response. Impulse control is crucial. Patience is a virtue.

Moving past red herrings requires massive emotional discipline to respond with relaxed, assertive confidence and take control of the conversation. So you need a simple framework that keeps you in control of emotional impulses—PAIS (Figure7.1):

Pause
Acknowledge
Ignore
Save

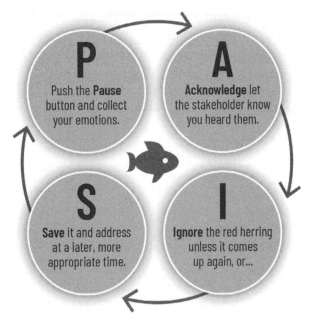

Figure 7.1   The PAIS Framework Helps You Move Past Red Herrings.

Pause: When your stakeholder attempts to draw you into a negotiation early, before they've selected you as their vendor of choice, pause and collect your emotions before speaking.

Acknowledge: Then let the stakeholder know that you heard them. You might say, "Before we jump right into pricing concerns, let's make sure our solution is even a good fit for you. May I ask a few questions so that I can better understand you and your organization?"

My favorite way to acknowledge a red herring is to simply take notes. Writing down what they say lets them know that I think it is important without getting pulled into giving away early concessions or my leverage.

Ignore or Save: When you pause and acknowledge, it creates enough space between the red herring and your response to make an intentional decision about your next move—whether you should ignore the red herring all together, save it and address it at a later point in the conversation, or in *rare cases* with transactional sales, when there are clear buying signals, proceed directly to closing the deal on the spot.

My default move is to ignore the red herring. I've learned, over a lifetime in the sales profession, that most early impulses to negotiate quickly fade once the stakeholder engages in the sales conversation. I simply acknowledge the concern or desire to negotiate, then I ask an unrelated open-ended question that gets them talking and telling their story.

Objections Versus Negotiation

Negotiation comes last in the sales process. Objections occur at multiple stages in the sales process.

Objections occur before you've won, before the stakeholder has selected you as their vendor of choice. Objections are questions, fear, worry, attachment to the status quo, and aversion to risk. They are roadblocks to advancing the deal.

Even though objections may sometimes feel like negotiations, they are not. It's important to know the difference, because failing to pay attention to the signs may cause you to negotiate at the wrong time.

If the stakeholder says "Your price is too high," it might be an objection or it might be an attempt at negotiation. This is when you must slow down and clarify what they mean, isolate it as their only concern, and either minimize the concern or gain agreement that if you can resolve the issue, they will choose you. *Then* negotiate.

If the stakeholder says "I love everything you've presented, and we're ready to get started, but we're going to need you to help us out on the price. What can we do?" then you've won, and it's time to negotiate.

(To learn more about the four types of sales objections you'll face in the sales process, read my book *Objections: The Ultimate Guide for Mastering the Art and Science of Getting Past No.*)

8 | Four Levels of Sales Negotiation

There are four levels of sales negotiation that impact the parameters under which the parties negotiate. Negotiation strategy shifts as the complexity and risk of the negotiated outcome to the parties increase.

Transactional

Transactional negotiation is basically haggling over a price. Preserving the relationship is not as important as preserving your price and margin. It's the type of negotiating you do when buying a car or an antique at a flea market.

Transactional negotiation is typically fast and furious. It's easy to walk away if the value is too low or the price too high. In transactional haggling, the emotional motivation to do a deal takes center stage. The person who wants the deal the most will make the most concessions.

1. Low risk.
2. Low to medium deal size—in some cases, such as high-volume commodity transactions, the deals may be large.
3. Price is the only issue at stake.
4. Relationship preservation is secondary to winning and getting a deal done.
5. A contest of emotional will and discipline.

Value-Add

Value-add is how companies change the shape of perceived commodities. Value-add negotiation includes both price and the terms and conditions for limited service delivery or add-on value like set up, installation, warranties, ongoing maintenance, etc. For example, if you were selling a piece of equipment, you might add on configuration and testing as part of the package.

The sales cycle is usually short for value-add sales. Typically, no formal contracts are involved other than purchase orders, bills of sale, or order forms. If there is a written agreement, it is short and sweet and contains limited and standard terms and conditions that do not require negotiation or are nonnegotiable.

Price takes center stage in the value-add sales negotiation, while terms and conditions may be used as leverage to maintain margin. Relationship preservation matters because you'll be providing value-added services and will want to protect the lifetime value of the relationship, which is likely to involve repeat purchases.

1. Low risk.
2. Low to medium deal size—in some cases, for instance with capital equipment, these deals may be large.

3. High weight on price.
4. Low weight on terms and conditions.
5. Terms and conditions are often used as leverage (value trade) to maintain margin.
6. Preserving the long-term relationship is a consideration to protect repeat purchases.

Complex

Complex deals involve longer sales cycles and, in many cases, multiple stakeholders. These deals typically involve contracts with complex terms and conditions. Because of this, price and terms and conditions are often weighted equally. For example, a five-year business services agreement valued at $500,000 that includes annual price increases, service level guarantees, and an evergreen clause.

Price is most often negotiated first, then terms and conditions. The price negotiation phase is usually rapid, while the negotiation on terms and conditions can drag on—especially when legal or procurement gets involved.

When you are negotiating a complex deal, your effectiveness during the discovery phase of the sales process is the key to winning for your team. Your leverage comes from your understanding of the stakeholder group's desired business outcomes, the implications of those outcomes, the implications of waiting or doing nothing, the implication of a failed solution, and the metrics that matter (MTMs) for their business.

Because these deals have long-term consequences for both parties, they carry much higher risk than transactional and value-add deals. Because these deals also involve long-term relationships, protecting the relationship is likewise important.

1. Medium to high-risk.
2. Multiple stakeholders.

3. Medium to high deal size.
4. Equal weight on price and terms and conditions.
5. Business case is focused on business outcome implications and MTMs.
6. Preserving long-term relationships is very important.

Enterprise

Enterprise-level deals involve massive risks to all parties. These deals are large in size; require long, arduous sales cycles that involve a wide array of stakeholders; and can be company-changing events. They involve intricate contracts and complex terms and conditions, and there are potential negative implications should either party breach the terms of the agreement.

Because of this, terms and conditions take center stage and will be the main focus of the sales negotiation. The economics of the deal are still important—but not nearly as important as getting alignment on terms and conditions. More often than not, the economics of the deal are woven into and cannot be separated from the terms and conditions. For example, a cloud-based digital transformation consulting agreement for a multinational company may require years of work by dozens of people who will be deeply embedded in the prospect's business and a pricing structure designed around performance milestones and measurable business outcomes.

The long sales and buying process involves vetting multiple vendors—most often via a formal RFP process. There is relative parity among competing vendors that leads to transparency around price, which makes raw price itself a lower priority at the negotiation table. Instead, total cost of ownership, measurable business outcomes, and return on investment carry more weight.

The terms and conditions negotiation can drag on for months and will, more often than not, be in the hands of legal or procurement—sometimes both.

When you are negotiating an enterprise-level deal, your effectiveness at developing a coach and/or executive sponsor along with relationships with other key stakeholders is crucial to your ability to negotiate favorable terms and conditions. You'll improve your power position by developing a strong executive sponsor who is willing to advocate for you and remove procurement's alternatives when you are facing maximum pressure.

1. Massive risk—mistakes may have extreme consequences.
2. Extremely large deal size.
3. Wide array of stakeholders.
4. Terms and conditions weighted higher than price.
5. A strong business case centered on measurable business outcomes (MBOs), along with a deep relationship with the stakeholder group, strengthens your power position.
6. Relationship preservation is essential.

With both complex and enterprise-level deals, excellence across the entire sales process is the real key to winning for your team. You must build a rock-solid business case for why you are the only vendor that can deliver on the stakeholder group's desired business outcomes and expected return on investment.

Sales Negotiation Parameters

We'll discuss the implications of understanding sales negotiation parameters in an upcoming chapter. What's important to note, though, is that the parameters of the negotiation should guide your strategy and tactics as you approach the sales negotiation table. These parameters will also play a significant role on the sales negotiation chess board as both parties jockey for leverage and power position.

NEGOTIATION PARAMETERS									
YOUR NEGOTIATION PARAMETERS	LOW	MEDIUM	HIGH	CRITICAL	THEIR NEGOTIATION PARAMETERS	LOW	MEDIUM	HIGH	CRITICAL
RISK PROFILE					RISK PROFILE				
VALUE					VALUE				
PRICING/ECONOMICS					PRICING/ECONOMICS				
TERMS & CONDITIONS					TERMS & CONDITIONS				
RELATIONSHIP					RELATIONSHIP				

Figure 8.1   Sales Negotiation Parameters.

PART

III

Sales Negotiation Strategy: Motivation, Leverage, and Power

9 | MLP Strategy

Sales negotiation is part chess match, part poker game, and part Sales EQ. It's strategic and a tactical.

Both parties have a list of desired outcomes. The buyer is making a purchase to eliminate pain, solve a problem, take advantage of an opportunity, and ultimately to generate a measurable business outcome and return on investment. The seller wishes to make a profit, generate growth, earn commissions and bonuses, and help their buyer achieve their desired outcomes.

Your mission is win for your team while protecting the relationship. The buyer is focused on procuring the best possible price, terms, and conditions, often with little regard for the relationship.

In most situations, the buyer has a stronger power position and more negotiation leverage than you. But there will be plenty of cases when you are in a position of strength, have leverage, and have enough opportunities in your pipeline to dampen your motivation to make concessions.

Motivation, leverage, and power position (MLP) are the chess board of sales negotiation. From the moment you engage a prospect until the proverbial ink is dry on the contract, your imperative is to analyze, influence, and shape the stakeholder group's MLP. In turn, you must be aware of and honest about your MLP and the gaps that put you at a disadvantage at the sales negotiation table. This is where sales negotiation strategy begins.

Figure 9.1   MLP Strategy.

10 | Motivation

My client engaged us for a consulting project to help them develop an account management process for their growing sales team. Their field-based hunter salesforce had been gaining market share rapidly, and they'd become accustomed to double-digit growth.

Suddenly, though, growth had slowed, and there was a sinking realization that they had a problem. The sales team had sold so many new accounts that they'd become bogged down servicing them and had stopped hunting for new opportunities.

We identified a firm timeline for completing the project. That timeline was tied to hiring and standing up an account management team, training them, and integrating them into the organization. The stakeholder group had selected my company, Sales Gravy, as the vendor of choice (VOC). The contract was sent to procurement to get ironed out.

That's when things bogged down. Procurement immediately asked us for price concessions. We refused, because we'd priced the deal so that we could deliver the business outcome required by the stakeholder group.

Procurement's gambit at that point was to stall and slow down communication. They insinuated that they had other alternatives (a power play). They were counting on our side to be motivated to get the deal done because we'd naturally want the revenue to start flowing.

Weeks went by. But we were in no hurry. We had an overflowing pipeline, along with multiple projects already underway. We were more worried about how to absorb this new project and get it done than closing the deal. Because of this, procurement's stalling tactic was welcomed.

In the meantime the pressure on the stakeholder group to find a solution for the problem was increasing. They were becoming agitated and started calling us almost daily to find out when we could start. The stakeholders' motivation to get a deal done was high. They even asked if we could get started while the terms of the contract were being worked out.

We politely explained that though we were anxious to get started, we needed the contract in place before we could begin. "We were just waiting on procurement to send over the final agreement—they were probably just backed up with workload."

As the stakeholder group realized that the deal was being held up on their end, our executive sponsor of the project—a senior vice president—made a call to the procurement team, and suddenly we had an inked contract on our terms. Motivation is a powerful thing.

The More You Want It

Here is a simple yet powerful truth. The more a party wants or needs an outcome, the more motivated they are to make concessions to get that outcome. For you, it means that the more you want the deal, the more you'll give up in order to ink it.

Motivation is a compelling reason, enthusiasm, drive, or desire for doing something. It comes in many different forms. People can be motivated by a time crunch, relationships, a desired future state, the fear of failure, the need to achieve, the desire to escape pain or suffering, to gain pleasure, to feel significance, financial gain, saving face, attachment, self-worth, satisfaction, and contentment.

Motivation Is Personal

What you must always remember is that motivation is personal. Particularly in business-to-business sales situations, you will be dealing with stakeholders who are using someone else's money to solve their problems. Each stakeholder will have their own unique and personal criteria for success—often diverging from that of the group or their organization.

These stakeholders' personal criteria for success, along with their relationship with you (and other members of your team), shape their motivation to get a deal done.

Motivation typically has an inverse correlation to power. Power in sales negotiations is directly correlated to the number of alternatives a party has.

Motivation is emotional and at times illogical. Because of this, it can be leveraged to neutralize and diminish the value of other alternatives. For example, if people really want to do business with *you*, then they'll allow their confirmation bias to guide them and ignore other possibilities.

The higher a stakeholder group's motivation to buy from you, the less attractive the perceived alternatives. This causes the stakeholder group's power position to weaken. The important thing to understand is that power (alternatives) is concentrated at the organizational level, while motivation is with the individual stakeholder.

In almost every deal, the company you are selling to is in a stronger power position than you because they have more alternatives. Therefore, to weaken the organization's power position at the negotiating table while strengthening yours, you must work to increase each individual stakeholder's motivation to get a deal done with *you*.

Increasing stakeholder motivation while reducing the perception of viable alternatives occurs on three levels:

1. Relationship
2. Individual success criteria
3. Social proof

The cumulative motivation of the various stakeholders in the deal will either increase or decrease the strength of perceived alternatives to selecting you and your company as the vendor of choice (VOC).

Relationship and the Decision Process

There are three processes in sales that, when aligned, result in sales negotiation serendipity. In fact, when the *sales*, *buying*, and *decision* processes are perfectly aligned, you rarely need to negotiate.

The sales process (you) and buying process (your prospect) are linear, rational steps developed at the organizational level. Your company has a sales process, and your prospect has a buying process.

The decision process, on the other hand, is individual, emotional, nonlinear, and often irrational—in essence, each stakeholder's personal buying journey. The decision process is how individual stakeholders commit to advocating for vendors, products, services, next steps, and, most importantly, the salesperson. It's where the motivation to do business with *you* is born.

The Five Questions That Matter Most

In every sales conversation, in each interaction, and throughout the sales process, stakeholders are asking five questions of you:

- Do I like you?
- Do you listen to me?
- Do you make me feel important?
- Do you get me and my problems?
- Do I trust and believe you?

These are the five most important questions in sales. These questions are being asked and answered by the stakeholders, consciously and subconsciously, as they interact with you. The questions are emotional. They originate from emotion and are answered with emotion.

How you answer these questions for each stakeholder will increase or decrease their motivation to advocate for you. When you answer the five questions in the affirmative it becomes almost impossible for them not to choose you as their preferred vendor.

Strategy Meets Tactics

One undeniable fact cannot be discounted or overlooked. As you advance through the sales and buying process, the most consistent predictor of outcome—more than any other variable—is the emotional experience of the stakeholder group while working with you.

In other words, the tangible attributes of a product or solution are less important to individual stakeholder motivation than emotional experience.

The decision process is where strategy meets tactics. Shaping the decision process allows you to leverage the relationships individual stakeholders have with you to weaken the organization's power position at the sales negotiation table. You accomplish this when you systematically and methodically engineer and execute the sales process so you interact with and influence the right stakeholders at the right time, and in the right situation.

As you advance through the sales process, you must engage each stakeholder and reach below the surface to understand their unique motivations, desires, needs, wants, fears, aspirations, and problems. You must use empathy to step into each individual's shoes and connect with them emotionally.

Effective negotiators are masters at aligning the sales process, buying process, and decision process. They never forget that they are dealing with emotional, fallible, irrational human beings. They know that through strong emotional connections, they develop advocates who help move win probabilities into the stratosphere, create unassailable competitive differentiation, and remove perceived alternatives.

BASIC: Stakeholder Mapping

You will be negotiating with people. Irrational humans who make decisions based on emotion. These stakeholders are driven by motivation to succeed, aversion to risk, confirmation biases, ego, fear, and a host of disruptive emotions—*just like you*.

There are five types of stakeholders: **B**uyers, **A**mplifiers, **S**eekers, **I**nfluencers, and **C**oaches—**BASIC** (Figure 10.1).

In small deals, you may be dealing with a single stakeholder or a few stakeholders playing multiple roles. In complex and enterprise-level deals, the stakeholder array will be wide. The stakeholder array will grow with:

1. Increased risk to the organization
2. Heightened risk to the individual stakeholders
3. Complexity of the product or service
4. Value of the deal
5. Length of the sales cycle
6. Size of the organization

Figure 10.1   BASIC: The Five Stakeholders.

Effective sales negotiators leave nothing to chance. Beginning with early-stage prospecting, through qualifying, and into discovery, they are identifying and mapping BASIC.

Each stakeholder has a "stake" in the outcome of the deal—motivated by personal desires, individual success criteria, and organizational requirements. Individual stakeholders may potentially give you information that improves your leverage or reveals their own or another stakeholder's motivation to make a deal. In conversations, they can and will reveal the organization's perceived alternatives, which gives you the opportunity to neutralize those alternatives and improve your power position.

Buyers

Buyers are decision makers—people with the ultimate authority to say yes or no. There are two types of buyers:

- **Commitment Buyer**—a person who can authorize the deal, sign a contract, and say yes to the commitment.

- **Funding Buyer**—a person who can authorize payment, issue a purchase order, and "write the check."

Sometimes these stakeholders are the same person, and other times they are not. For example:

- The CIO may be able to say yes to a new software purchase, but until the CFO agrees to release the funds, nothing will happen.
- A corporate purchaser can say yes to your terms, while general managers at field locations can say yes to approving the budget.
- The stakeholder group can select you as the vendor of choice, while procurement will approve the pricing and terms of the deal.

Understanding this difference will save you the pain and anguish of negotiating with people who do not have the authority to say yes or getting ink on a deal only to see the revenue fail to materialize.

In best-case scenarios, you should be negotiating with the funding buyer. In all cases, your goal should be to get the funding buyer in the room.

You want to avoid negotiating a deal with the commitment buyer or an influencer, only to find yourself making even more concessions to their counterpart who holds the purse strings later. When big concessions are on the line, use your leverage to get everyone "in the room."

Amplifiers

Amplifiers are stakeholders who see a problem or gap that your product or service can fill. They are typically lower-level people who will either use or be impacted by your product or service. Leveraged well, they become advocates for change and amplify the message, problem, pain, or need up through the organization.

In most cases, their influence on the outcome of the deal is indirect. Effective sales negotiators are masters at leveraging the amplifiers' pain or their advocacy to remove the alternative of *doing nothing* from the table. If enough amplifiers voice their pain, it is difficult for other stakeholders to make no decision.

Seekers

Seekers are stakeholders sent to look for information early in the buying process. They download e-books, attend webinars, peruse websites, and fill out web forms. Seekers rarely have buying authority or influence, yet they put up a façade of authority and block access to other stakeholders. Sadly, salespeople go for this ruse hook, line, and sinker; in doing so, they set themselves up for failure in the negotiation stage, because they give away their leverage to the seeker early and for free.

Influencers

Influencers are stakeholders that play an active role in the buying process. The have a say at the negotiation table. In complex and enterprise-level sales, you will spend most of your time with influencers. They come in three flavors:

- **Advocates** are on your side. They are motivated to choose you as the preferred vendor. Strong advocates will work on your behalf to remove potential alternatives to doing business with you. You must work actively to nurture and cultivate advocates because the more advocates you have, the stronger your power position.
- **Agnostics** go with the flow. They have the tendency to follow the crowd—either because they are motivated by self-preservation, uninterested, or are not impacted by the decision. Your imperative with agnostics is to get below the surface and understand their personal motivations and success criteria. If self-preservation is their motive, you must find a way to give

them cover. If they feel they are not impacted or if they are uninterested, you must work to give them an emotional or business reason to become motivated to participate. The danger with agnostics is that they are easily swayed by the opinions of naysayers. You must never lose sight of this imminent danger.

- **Naysayers** are against you, your company, or change. They kill deals, push alternatives, and actively work against you. You cannot argue a naysayer into believing that they are wrong. When you push and argue, they dig in and work even harder to sabotage your position. Instead of arguing, focus on neutralizing them. You'll accomplish this through empathy, listening, and investing in a relationship with the naysayer. In addition, you'll want to focus on developing and building stronger ties with advocates, who in numbers and veracity can shut naysayers down.

Coaches

Coaches, champions, and executive sponsors are insiders who are willing to advocate for you, help you with insider information, and remove barriers to negotiated outcomes.

They give you information that helps you improve your power position, work with you to neutralize naysayers, align stakeholder groups, facilitate communication, and let you know when an implicit choice has been made by the stakeholder group for you—when you've won.

Executive sponsors and champions can improve your power position with funding buyers (especially procurement) by being clear that you are the only alternative. In any complex deal, developing a coach and/or executive sponsor is a huge advantage at the sales negotiation table.

The Stakeholder Negotiation List and Motivation Scale

In every deal, the stakeholders have a list. This list includes their personal success criteria, hopes, wishes, wants, needs, desired business outcomes, metrics that matter, must-haves, deal-breakers, and core motivations. Knowing the stakeholders' negotiation lists reduces surprises while improving your leverage and power position at the sales negotiation table.

Effective sales negotiators begin compiling the stakeholder negotiation list from the very beginning of the sales process. You'll build the stakeholder negotiation list primarily in the qualification and discovery phases of the sales process. Start by answering these five questions:

1. What are the success criteria of each key stakeholder?
2. What does each stakeholder specifically want?
3. What problem(s) are they trying to solve?
4. What are the emotional and measurable business outcomes (MBOs) each stakeholder expects from this deal, and how will they measure them?
5. What are their nonnegotiables or deal-breakers?

Building this list helps you understand where there are gaps in your knowledge, where you have work to do to get stakeholders on your side, what the potential conflicts with your own list, and where there is common ground. The stakeholder negotiation list acts as a roadmap for eliminating perceived alternatives that do not check the boxes on the list and building your Give–Take Playlist (see Chapter 26).

You'll build the stakeholder negotiation list organically through both formal and informal conversations with the stakeholder group. Step into each stakeholder's shoes and view things from their perspective.

1. What are their motivations?
2. What does success look like to them?
3. What problems are they trying to solve?
4. What is the risk to them personally if they choose you?
5. What is the risk if they do not choose you?
6. Why might they advocate for you?
7. Why might they be a naysayer?
8. What are their emotional hot buttons?

9. What makes them feel important? How can you tap into this?
10. What do they fear?
11. What is their ideal agreement and relationship with your company?
12. What are the budgetary limitations or conflicts?
13. What are the important terms and conditions?
14. What are their expectations when working with your company and vendors like your company?

Get Over Your Fear and Get Issues on the Table Early

The key is leveraging strategic and artful questions that force stakeholders to put their negotiation list and nonnegotiables on the table early. This way you can confront, sidestep, or neutralize alternatives and deal-breakers before you enter the negotiation phase.

Of course, this is easier said than done. It requires tact and nuance to pull this type of information out of stakeholders.

The challenge salespeople face in surfacing stakeholder issues, however, is not the stakeholder's unwillingness to answer the questions. Rather, it's the salesperson's own disruptive emotions that hold them back.

Humans—you, me, and most other people—are sensitive to conflict and the potential for rejection. Avoiding conflict is why we hesitate and shy away from asking questions that get the truth on the table. Salespeople hide behind justifications for not asking for the truth. They say they don't want to "seem too pushy" or that "the timing was bad." There is always the potential that you will get shut down, which hurts.

But avoiding questions that bring the truth to the surface is a wickedly stupid sales negotiation strategy. It leads to delusion, and in sales you cannot be delusional and successful at the same time. When you choose delusion over awareness, you are making a conscious choice not only to lie to yourself but to limit your ability to negotiate effectively and get ink.

Nothing is more dangerous than going into a sales negotiation unprepared and uninformed, without a clear view of the other side's negotiation list. It is debilitating when a stakeholder blindsides you late in the negotiation stage with a demand you did not know was simmering below the surface.

The Trouble with Stakeholders

Of course, getting your stakeholders' issues, concerns, worries, budget, limitations, demands, and nonnegotiables on the table is not easy. Stakeholders:

- Operate at the emotional level.
- Avoid conflict and therefore hold back information, obfuscate, and use smoke screens to obscure their real concerns.
- Don't always know what they want or their limitations.
- Are sometimes unable to articulate problems, success criteria, or their vision of the ideal agreement.
- Hide the truth because they feel that being transparent weakens their position.

As a result, identifying the other side's negotiation list is like putting together a jigsaw puzzle. Throughout the sales process, you must be asking questions, listening, paying attention to emotional cues and nuance, and assembling your stakeholder negotiation list one piece at a time. It is not and never will be a perfect science.

Aligning Decision Making with Social Proof

As the complexity of the sale, the length of the cycle, and, more importantly, the risk to the organization and individual stakeholders increase, so does size of the stakeholder array. With more stakeholders in the mix, the risk to the individual stakeholders is diluted while the risk to you is increased.

With a large array of stakeholders playing different roles (BASIC), it's easier for stakeholders to act on groupthink rather than standing up for a view that might be the right thing but be perceived as unpopular. It's also easier for a single stakeholder (usually a naysayer) to derail a deal when the stakeholder group is indecisive or misaligned. It's less risky for the group to be cautious and *do nothing* instead of taking a risk and being wrong.

What we know empirically about human behavior is that humans avoid risk and follow the crowd. We are compelled and motivated to do things that other people are doing. When something is popular, when we see other people doing it, we feel that it is safe to do the same thing.

This is the social proof bias. The more people doing a thing, having a belief in something, or sharing an opinion, the higher the probability is that we'll be drawn toward and want to do or believe the same thing.

We use the judgment of the crowd as substitute for our own. This reduces cognitive load, making it easier to make quick decisions in complex environments.

In complex deals with wide stakeholder arrays, you improve your power position by leveraging social proof. The key is mobilizing amplifiers and advocates to neutralize naysayers and swing agnostics to your side.

Stakeholder alignment is hard work. It requires:

- Sales process strategy and execution
- Stakeholder mapping
- Disciplined efforts to identify and contact all stakeholders
- Intentional efforts to build relationships with even the most hostile stakeholders (it's harder for them to throw you under the bus when they like you)
- Never assuming that stakeholders are talking to each other or like each other
- Taking an active role in communicating stakeholder agreement, common ground, and organizing consensus up, down, and across the stakeholder array

You cannot leave anything to chance. You need to have a level of paranoia that there is a stakeholder you have not identified waiting in the weeds to sink your deal. You must not assume that communication with and among stakeholders is equivalent to agreement.

Social proof is especially powerful when the stakeholders are right on the cusp of choosing you but may be questioning whether the outcomes you've promised will materialize or the process of implementing your solution will disrupt their business.

This is where case studies, written testimonials, references, and referenceable and measurable business outcomes (RMBOs) from other similar customers help to minimize the perceived risk and make it easier for you to neutralize naysayers, sway agnostics, and give advocates the cover they need to move forward.

It is important to note, though, that there is not a social proof fairy. It doesn't materialize on its own. If you work for a large company, the marketing department will surely provide you with some case studies and social proof marketing material. The problem is that it's usually generic and one-size-fits-all material.

Social proof works best when it comes from people or businesses that are like your stakeholder group and inside their familiarity bubble. RMBOs from similar organizations are powerful social proof.

I once sold a service that most of my prospects already used. My primary focus, therefore, was displacing the incumbent vendor. The fear that the transition from one vendor to the other would be a disruptive disaster made *doing nothing* seem like a viable alternative for the stakeholders. It was also my competitor's strongest card to play to weaken my position.

To neutralize this fear, I presented testimonials from my customers that included specific RMBOs. In these letters my customers gushed about how smoothly the transition went and how this made it easier for them to rapidly achieve measurable business outcomes. It was all the ammunition I needed to get stakeholder groups lining up to select me as their VOC.

My process for getting the testimonials was simple:

1. I took ownership and made sure the installations went well.
2. I asked my happy customers if they would provide a testimonial—they almost always gave me an emphatic yes.
3. I wrote the testimonial for them. This was key to getting them to do it, because if I left it to my customers to write them, it would never happen.
4. I emailed the testimonial I'd prepared and asked them for permission to use it with their logo and/or headshot.
5. I followed up to make sure they followed through. People are busy, and sometimes you must remind them of their commitment.

The result was a social proof tool I used to bludgeon my competitors and strengthen my power position.

You must be intentional and systematic about building social proof tools that help your buyers trust you to deliver on your promises. You must systematically ask for testimonials and LinkedIn recommendations, collect case studies that profile RMBOs, and nurture references. Don't wait for someone else to do this for you, and don't be shy about asking. If you don't ask, you won't get.

In complex deals with wide stakeholder arrays, effective sales negotiators become a communication hub that connects the stakeholder group. This provides the social proof that helps stakeholders feel comfortable advocating for you.

Everything effective sales negotiators do at the strategic and tactical level all the way through the sales process is directed toward influencing stakeholder motivation. *Everything.*

This is the real key to strengthening your power position at the sales negotiation table. Take shortcuts here, and you'll get crushed.

Use more social proof how?

11 | Leverage

When you have something that someone else wants, you have leverage. You may use leverage to compel people to:

- Change their behavior
- Lean in and engage
- Move toward your position
- Make concessions
- Stop negotiating and align on an agreement

Let's reiterate a basic truth about sales negotiation. In most cases, organizations and their stakeholders are in a stronger power position than you—because they almost always have more alternatives.

The party with more power is in a position to exert more control over the buying process and extract more concessions at the sales negotiation table. At times, a party may perceive or know that they have so much power that they need not make any concessions or compromises and therefore become intractable—"do business on my terms or else!"

Leverage gives either party in the deal, regardless of power position, the ability to compel the other party to change a behavior. For the party in the weaker power position—with fewer alternatives—leverage preservation takes on strategic importance. It is in the weaker party's best interest to hold on tightly to leverage and then use it at the right moments to compel the stronger party to bend to their will.

Leverage is currency, and it must be treated as such. It has value and must be exchanged for value. Effective sales negotiators never give away leverage without getting something of equal or greater value in return. From the moment you engage a prospect until the deal is inked, you should never give leverage away for free. The types of leverage come in many forms including:

- Information
- Terms and conditions
- Pricing
- Sunk-cost fallacy
- Cognitive dissonance
- The human need for significance
- Scarcity
- Trust
- Motivation
- Time
- Urgency
- Relationship preservation
- Measurable business outcomes
- FOMO
- Free stuff
- Additional services

You will use leverage in two distinct ways when working with stakeholders:

1. As negotiation leverage to gain alignment on an agreement at the sales negotiation table.
2. Bending the buying process to your sales process in order to gain control so that you may eliminate or neutralize alternatives.

Using Leverage to Gain Alignment and Get Ink

In the back and forth of the sales negotiation table, leverage is used in value trades that help you to get a deal done while protecting your profit margins and hence your commission check.

This, of course, means that you must know and understand what levers drive profit for your company, and how and why they work. Profit drivers include:

- Certain high-margin products and services
- Product and service add-ons and ancillary products
- Agreement length
- Agreement terms
- Payment terms
- Future price increases
- Minimums
- Standardized product specs
- Standardized service requirements
- Geographic service area
- Compliance requirements
- Guarantees

This is a partial list, and every organization is different. It is your responsibility to understand what drives profit for your organization and how. Further, you need to understand how profit levers impact your income.

As an example, one company I sold for paid ten times more for a five-year agreement than for a two-year agreement because the profit margins increased exponentially after year two. Signing a three-, four-, or five-year agreement could mean the difference between making $10,000 or $1,000 in commission. I always entered negotiations asking for a five-year agreement and was prepared to give concessions on less profitable items like account set-up charges in exchange for more time on the agreement.

It's all about value, and value, of course, is in the eye of the beholder. The key is paying attention to what stakeholders focus on and what they perceive to be valuable (see the earlier discussion of the stakeholder negotiation list).

At the sales negotiation table, when the other side asks for a concession—your leverage—you must always ask for something in exchange. For example, if the buyer says that they don't want to pay the mandatory professional services fee, you may agree to remove the fee in exchange for an extra year on the contract agreement to "give them more time to do it on their own."

It's a simple value exchange. If you give leverage away, you should receive something in return of equal or greater value.

It's important to understand that what is valuable to your stakeholder might be less valuable to you. But that does not change the value of the leverage to gain concessions or compel the buyer to stop negotiating and align on an agreement and ink the deal.

For example, they may value having your janitorial team cleaning their offices on Wednesdays, but which day of the week you serve them may make no difference to you. In the negotiation, this gives you leverage. If you want them to agree to a certain contract condition, you might trade "guaranteed Wednesday service days" for that concession.

This is why you must treat leverage just as you would treat hard-earned money. It's precious and scarce, and it must be saved and protected so that you have it at your disposal when you need to compel the other side to move off their position and toward yours. We'll discuss how to build a negotiation leverage inventory and develop a Give-Take Playlist (GTP) in greater detail in an Chapter 26.

Using Leverage to Align the Buying Process to Your Sales Process

This spring I caught one of my salespeople as she was just about to give away a big piece of her leverage for free. We were in the early stages of a potentially monster training deal. The prospect is a Fortune 50 company seeking a training partner to help them with prospecting and top-of-funnel strategies. Their sales enablement team engaged us because they'd heard about the success of our Fanatical Prospecting Boot Camps.

Following the second discovery meeting, they'd asked for a presentation on our training methodology and an overview of our curriculum before they would agree to level us up to the executive who was the ultimate decision maker. It was a classic move by influencers to retain power. Even though this was not the ideal advance for us, we bent to their will because their leverage—a meeting with the decision maker—was stronger than ours. We had no other choice if we planned to continue advancing the deal.

My sales rep and her manager spent three days building and customizing the presentation. I stopped by to check on how it was going. She responded, "We'll be ready to email it over in the morning."

"Whoa!" I said. Alarms were going off in my head. "We don't give leverage away for free."

At first, she wasn't tracking. It seemed perfectly normal to comply with the stakeholder's request to email over our presentation.

"What happens after you send her the presentation?" I asked.

Silence, thinking, searching for a response. But there was none. She knew the truth. After she emailed the presentation (our leverage) and the stakeholder had what she wanted, the likelihood that the deal would go dark and stall was high.

"How many hours have you sunk into crafting this presentation?"

"At least ten?" she muttered.

"So, you've invested all of this time and effort. And now you plan to email the presentation without getting anything in return?" I was shaking my head in disapproval. "What should you be asking for?"

I stared at her in disbelief for a moment before she realized the mistake she was on the edge of making. Being eager to please nice stakeholders is a disruptive emotion. Eagerness is happy to reach into your back pocket and give away all of your leverage.

"I should ask them to schedule a meeting to review the proposal and use it as a stepping-stone to level up to the decision maker."

"Exactly!" I responded. "You have leverage. Use it to bend their process to our process. Use it to test their engagement. Use it to get a micro-commitment. Use it to make them match your effort."

My rep made the call and asked for a meeting to review her presentation and walk them through the curriculum. They agreed.

The presentation opened up a robust conversation. They told us that they did not want to attempt to build this type of training in-house (strike one alternative) and that our curriculum aligned much more closely with their vision than the other training provider they were considering (strike another alternative).

The stakeholder group was impressed enough that they agreed to set up a meeting to allow us to share the presentation with the decision maker—a micro-commitment that advanced the deal.

Mapping the Buying Process

Most large companies have a formally defined process for buying. Smaller organizations, at a minimum, have an informal buying process. The buying process typically has checks and balances to ensure that the company's stakeholders are making good decisions with the company's money.

Typically, the more complex the sale, the more formal and thoroughly defined the buying process. In low-complexity, low-risk, and short-cycle situations, the buying process will often involve a single person (perhaps the business owner) making a simple yes or no decision or an informal "Before we do anything, we have to review it with Mary."

When you are working complex and enterprise-level deals, it is imperative that you understand the organization's formal buying process. You'll need to know the steps that are involved and the stakeholders' expectations and timing for moving through those steps. Nailing down and mapping the buying process isn't easy or cut-and-dried.

- Stakeholders may obscure the process because they feel doing so gives them a negotiating advantage.
- Sometimes stakeholders don't have access to the bigger picture, and you may only uncover isolated slices of the process that leave out vital steps.
- In other cases, stakeholders have a difficult time walking you through their buying process because they don't view it as a process.
- Sometimes, they make it up as they go.

It is imperative that you ask about the process and keep asking. Once you understand how the organization buys, you can begin applying leverage to *bend* its buying process to align with your sales process. This is the first step in gaining control and starting the systematic, step-by-step process of strengthening your power position.

One of the most effective tactics for aligning the sales and buying processes is gaining consensus and agreement during the initial meeting on steps that both parties must advance through for a tailored proposal to be delivered.

The proposal is your business case and pricing—the formal offer to the buyer that serves as the upper limit anchor in the sales negotiation. It is also your most powerful leverage in the sales process, because it is the information stakeholders want most. They've invested time with you throughout the sales process, and the proposal is their reward. You may use it without impunity to obligate buyers to bend their process to yours.

Do Not Email Proposals *ask Sam*

Proposals are *never* emailed. If stakeholders want your information, they *must* schedule a formal proposal meeting to get it. When I see salespeople emailing proposals to stakeholders, it's like fingernails on a chalk board to me.

You must never, never, never deliver a proposal via email or any other means that keeps you from being there to walk your buyer through it. Why? Because a proposal is a formal offer. It's the platform on which you present your business case and *ask* for the sale. It's your opportunity to get an explicit decision, ink the deal, or begin the sales negotiation process.

Yes, of course, the sales negotiation will extend far beyond this meeting on larger, enterprise-level deals. Even then, though, there are usually some items on the stakeholder negotiation list that can be locked down in this meeting.

If you are not there by phone, video stream, or in person, none of this happens. More often than not, your proposal goes into a black hole, and you are left chasing stakeholders down with futile "just checking in" calls.

Worse, your business case may be interpreted the wrong way or taken out of context. Since you are not there to gauge their reactions and clarify these misunderstandings, that impression sticks. This may open up potential alternatives and put you in a weaker position.

Stakeholders Use Leverage to Make Salespeople Dance

Far too often, salespeople, like my rep, get pulled into the prospect's buying process and are told to dance. And, rather than using their leverage to gain control, salespeople dance.

They rush headlong into these deals, producing proposals, pitching solutions in the absence of information, challenging before understanding, blind to the influence of other stakeholders, and asking for commitments without earning the right. Because the buying process and sales process are out of sync, they skip steps, allow disruptive emotions to drive their behaviors, and push situational awareness aside.

In the process, their win probability plummets, and the outcomes are predictable.

- Deals stall and resources are wasted on pursuing low-probability deals.
- Salespeople negotiate with themselves.
- Time is wasted on deals that never close.
- Leaders are frustrated because pipelines are unpredictable.
- Stakeholders are exasperated because they waste time in shallow, low-value conversations.
- Valuable concessions are made in an attempt to cover up for these mistakes and gain the business.

If you've been in sales for more than a month, a prospect has said these words (or something similar) to you in person, on the phone, or via email:

- "I'm too busy to meet now, but we are interested. Just send me your proposal. I'll look it over and call you back to set a meeting."
- "Send over your prices; we're always looking for a better deal. Make sure you sharpen your pencil."
- "I'm gathering all the information from vendors. Once we get it all in, we'll start scheduling meetings."
- "We're going to be making a decision this week, so we need to get your information fast. How soon can you send us your proposal?"

You must not give in to the disruptive emotions of eagerness and desperation and react. To do so is to give away your leverage for free. Instead, protect your leverage and use it to gain control and bend their buying process to your sales process.

In all of these cases, your leverage is information. The buyer wants or needs your information (read pricing or free consulting). If you acquiesce to their request, you give away your leverage for free and become their puppet. Because once they have all of the leverage and the power, they, not you, are in control.

If, however, you trade your leverage (information) for a meeting, discovery call, or conversation with a decision maker, you have the chance to gain control and align their process with yours.

In complex and enterprise-level deals, buyers sometimes attempt to negotiate certain milestones in the sales process prematurely. For example, before a software demo, the buyer might say: "It's going to take a lot of work and investment to get our team together for the demo. I don't want to waste their time if your prices are too high. Please send over your best pricing and if it makes sense, we'll do the demo."

If the salesperson concedes, they give away their most powerful leverage for free and out of context. If they do manage to get through the process and later offer a final proposal, the buyer will come back seeking even more concessions.

This tactic is used by savvy buyers before moving forward with any number of next steps—demos, pilots, facility tours, discovery meetings, etc. Sometimes buyers say they need to see your prices before they'll even engage in an initial meeting.

If you give in to your emotions and give away your leverage, you immediately put yourself in a position of weakness. Frankly, it's most likely that your prices will go right into your competitor's hands, giving you no chance to close the deal.

The better move is to use your leverage to test engagement and get to the next step. For example:

Buyer: "We're looking forward to bringing our team on site to tour your facility. Before we take this next step, though, we want to take a look at your pricing structure."

Seller: "That makes sense. You certainly want to make sure we are a good fit before investing a lot of time in this process. (This uses the ledge technique that we'll discuss in Chapter 20.)

That's exactly why we want you and your team to visit our facility. This gives you a chance to meet our team and see exactly how we work. And, we'll have a chance to learn about your expectations and success criteria.

Once this visit is complete, we'll tailor a proposal around your unique situation. From there, both of us can then make an informed decision about whether or not it makes sense to keep talking. How about we set the tour up for next Thursday at 2 p.m.?"

The Curious Shape of Time

Time and the shape of time—speeding it up or slowing it down—is powerful leverage, especially when a party's motivation to ink a deal is high. Deadlines and urgency will pull concessions out of you and your stakeholders like nothing else.

Effective negotiators are masters at gaining consensus on a timeline for engagement from stakeholders early in the sales process. However, time leverage goes both ways. For example, your motivation goes up when you are backed up against a forecast commitment, contest deadline, or bonus opportunity.

I love it when buyers have deadlines. If they don't have a deadline, I do my level best to get them to commit to timelines during the discovery/demo phase of the sales process. Likewise (especially with transactional and short-cycle deals), special discounts, product scarcity, limited quantities, delivery timelines, potential back orders, etc. all create urgency, give you leverage, and, when they eliminate alternatives, strengthen your power position. Anything that creates urgency is kryptonite against power at the sales negotiation table.

Buyers have mastered the use of time to get salespeople to dance. I know buyers that purposely delay negotiating until right before the end of the quarter, because they know salespeople and their leaders are far more pliable then.

Take one of the previous examples: "We're going to be making a decision this week, so we need to get your information fast. How soon can you send us your proposal?" It's the old "speed you up to slow you down" play. The stakeholder indicates that they're interested and about to make a buying decision. "If you want in, you need to move fast."

This tactic is called time compression. Buyers tell salespeople they have a limited time for a shot at a deal or before a decision will be made. Salespeople go for it—hook, line, and sinker. They stop what they're doing, spend an afternoon (or an entire day) putting together the perfect proposal, push their leaders to approve lower prices, email the proposal, put the deal in the pipeline, add it to their forecast, and then hope.

Why does this happen? The salesperson fails to manage disruptive emotions—desperation, lack of confidence, fear of missing out (FOMO), and false hope.

Rather than reacting, respond to time compression, in all forms, with relaxed confidence. Explain your position and use leverage to compel the buyer to move toward you.

Buyer: "We're going to be making a decision this week, so we need to get your information fast. How soon can you send us your proposal?"

Seller: "John, my competitors will be happy to just throw a proposal at you. It's easy for them. They've got a generic box and expect all their customers to fit into that box. This is where we are different. At my company, we build the box around you. All I'm going to need is a little bit of your time to ask some questions so I can understand you better. Then I'll tailor a proposal around your unique situation. That way, you'll have the opportunity to make a true apples-to-apples comparison and choose the solution that you feel is best for your company. How about we get together tomorrow afternoon at two o'clock?"

When you use leverage this way, you'll get one of three possible responses:

"That makes sense—when can we meet?" At this point you have gained control, reshaped the buying process, and obtained the power to align it to the sales process—most likely disrupting a competitor's rep who believed he or she had the deal wrapped up.

"How much time will this take?" or **"Is there any other way we can do this?"** In this case the buyer is negotiating for your leverage. You learn that there is urgency, so you only need to work out how and when the discovery meeting will occur.

"Look, we really don't have time to meet. If you want a shot at this, send us your proposal." You now know that there is no chance for a deal. Walk away and preserve your precious time and leverage for a higher-probability play.

Effective sales negotiators don't scratch lottery tickets. They control disruptive emotions in pursuit of higher win probabilities. They never waste time filling out a blind RFP or delivering a "Hail Mary" proposal because of FOMO. Hope is not a strategy or a good investment of time.

Instead, effective negotiators use leverage to shape stakeholder behaviors and put themselves in position to win by shaping the prospect's buying process to align with their sales process.

Do not give your leverage away for free. One more time for the folks in the back of the room who are still not tracking—*do not give leverage away for free.* When you give value, you must ask for and get something of greater or equal value in return.

12 | Power Position

Power is derived from having alternatives. At the sales negotiation table, the more alternatives a party has, the stronger its power position. The more power a party has, the more concessions it can demand.

Buyers are almost always in a stronger power position than sellers.

- Buyers usually have the option of *doing nothing*—making no decision. *delaying decision*
- There is almost always a *competitor* waiting in line to sell them a similar product or service. *other planner*
- There may even be the option of taking it *in-house* and doing it themselves. *DIY*

Salespeople are typically in a weaker power position because they have fewer alternatives.

- They are working from thin to nonexistent pipelines because they fail to prospect consistently.
- They find themselves backed into the corner by leaders who demand that they make monthly, quarterly, and annual forecasts.
- They are on performance plans and must get deals done to remain employed.
- The competition in their market or industry is fierce.
- There are many similar offerings in the market that buyers perceive to be the same.
- Even though they almost always have another prospect to sell to, it rarely feels this way to salespeople.

Therefore, buyers naturally start off in a stronger power position, making it easy for them to persuade desperate salespeople in a weaker position to give away their leverage for free.

One part of the buyers' strength is the natural order of things. For example, if the buyer is a large multinational company with a premier brand name, it's likely that a long line of salespeople is waiting for a shot at a deal. Organizations with vast resources have massive purchasing and negotiating power.

A larger reason, though, is the sellers' self-inflicted wounds. Sellers imagine that the buyers have more options than they actually do. This false belief can be a result of the buyer's bluff or the seller's lack of knowledge about the marketplace and competitors. Often it is a symptom of poor discovery during the sales process that failed to uncover that the buyer needs the seller far more than they are letting on.

Your Singular Focus Is to Strengthen Your Power Position

You want to feel in control. You want to feel confident. You want to feel like you have power. You want to avoid making concessions that negatively impact your compensation.

This is why so many salespeople are looking for Obi-Wan Kenobi tactics that allow them to outmaneuver the other party with the wave of a hand: "These aren't the droids you're looking for."

That's the kind of power we all want. But, of course, that only happens in the movies (and some negotiation books and training courses that pander to this desire). The real secret to getting the "negotiation force" on your side, though, is not a sexy, cool Jedi mind trick. It's something much more boring.

You see, the most common reason salespeople find themselves in a weak power position is that they skipped steps or took short-cuts in the sales process. When you skip steps—*especially discovery*—in the sales process, you:

- Are forced to make concessions before you've won
- Become the buyer's puppet
- Get squeezed for maximum discounts but have no ammunition to defend and justify your position because you failed to do deep discovery and build a clear case for the value of your proposal
- Give deep discounts on your prices to compensate for the fact that you "showed-up-and-threwed-up"
- Waste time negotiating with stakeholders who cannot make decisions and end up negotiating for the same ground twice
- Have a weak business case and are unable to eliminate or neutralize the other party's alternatives

I can teach you sales negotiation mindsets, strategies, frameworks, and techniques until the cows come home. But if you take shortcuts in the sales process, you'll be right back where you started—frustrated, failing, discounting, and giving away your commission check.

Each day of my professional life, I'm approached by salespeople who are looking to me to give them Jedi mind tricks. They are desperately seeking the one killer technique that will turn them into masters of closing and negotiating.

These delusional salespeople refuse to face the truth that the real secret to mastering closing and sales negotiation begins with excellence throughout the sales process. For them, it is better to seek the shortcut, easy button, or a mystical mind trick than to buckle down and do the hard work, systematically and methodically advancing deals through the pipe step, by step, by step.

No negotiation technique, no move, no play, no gambit will save you from a failure to follow and execute the sales process. It's the fundamental reason salespeople give it all away at the negotiating table.

Sales Truth: It's the Sales Process, Stupid

You cannot separate excellence in the sales process from excellence in sales negotiation. As my buddy Mike Weinberg says, "That's the *Sales Truth*."

You are sick and tired of hearing about the sales process. I know. It sucks. You get this message in sales training. From your leaders in meetings and one to ones. You get it in books like this. It's boring, and salespeople hate boring.

You want something more. There's got to be more! Perhaps you're thinking to yourself as you read my admonition on following the sales process, "There's nothing new here. I've heard it all before. Sales process, sales process, sales process. Enough!"

You want a better way. You want me to pander to you and tell you that I have a technique that is guaranteed to make you a powerful negotiator and close the deal every time.

It's not going to happen. If any trainer or author tells you that you can take shortcuts in the sales process and still be an effective closer or negotiator, they're lying.

So, if you're pissed because I'm not telling you what you want to hear, get over it. Seeking shortcuts is a deliberate decision to fail. Hiding from the truth is pure delusion.

The real secret to inking deals and gaining *power* at the sales negotiating table is mastering, controlling, and executing the sales process. This is the most important lesson in this book. I hope you are tracking, because here's the brutal sales truth: *boring works.*

Jedi Mind Tricks

Sales outcomes are predictable, based on how salespeople leverage, execute, and move deals through the sales process. Follow a well-designed sales process with qualified prospects who are in the buying window, and you will close more deals at higher prices and more favorable terms and conditions. It's the truth, and it's a guarantee.

If you are looking for a Jedi mind trick that will give you the upper hand in negotiations with buyers, look no further than being excellent at (Figure 12.1):

1. Prospecting
2. Qualifying
3. Initial meetings
4. Aligning the sales and buying processes
5. Mapping stakeholders
6. Gaining consistent micro-commitments
7. Discovery, discovery, discovery
8. Solution mapping and stakeholder consensus
9. Value bridging, presentations, and proposals
10. Getting past objections
11. Negotiating
12. Locking it in with *Ink*

Figure 12.1 Success at Sales Means Putting the Pieces in Place in the Right Order.

Systematically putting qualified opportunities into your sales pipeline and advancing them though the pipeline are the keys to winning first and making sales negotiations exponentially easier. The sales process and the negotiation process are inextricably intertwined.

You cannot wait until you reach the negotiation stage to begin thinking about negotiating. To be effective, you must look at the entire chess board from the get-go with a focus on bending the probability that you win for your team in your favor. You must know the players, protect your leverage, improve your power position, and plan your moves.

In chess and in sales, every move has a win probability. It's a simple matter of mathematics—based on what's on the board. Calculating the win probability of each move is how professional chess masters and ultra–high-performing sales professionals play and win the game.

Every action, each step, every question, every word they utter, the demo, the presentation—everything they do along the sales process is calculated and designed to bend the win probability in their favor and improve their position when the time to negotiate comes.

In each sales situation, there will be multiple paths to ink and multiple techniques you can deploy. Like a chess master, you must choose the path that gives you the highest probability of getting a win for your team.

The Power Is in Alternatives

BATNA, or Best Alternative to a Negotiated Agreement, is a term coined by Roger Fisher and William Ury in their classic book, *Getting to Yes: Negotiating Without Giving In.*[1]

BATNA is your best alternative should you be unable to come to a negotiated agreement. For example, it could be walking away and finding another buyer, stripping the deal down to its skeleton, or the agreement you'd end up with if you conceded all the way down to your limit and nonnegotiable position.

The reason why stakeholders choose to negotiate is that they feel that negotiation will result in a better deal than not negotiating. Rather than blindly accepting your proposal and your word that it's a good deal, they ask you to make concessions.

When a party has viable alternatives, they have power, because they can emotionally detach and move on to another option. Generally, the more alternatives they feel they have, the more concessions they'll be able to extract.

In most cases, they'll have alternatives. For example, in all but a few situations the stakeholders have the option to do nothing. This is why "no decision"—sticking with the status quo—is the number-one reason deals are lost.

Some prospects may choose to do it themselves and take it in-house. This was the BATNA that I had in my back pocket when I was negotiating with a company to outsource my video editing and production. When we couldn't come to an agreement on price, I hired my own team.

Of course, the BATNA buyers most often wield as power is doing business with your competitors. There are almost always competitors, and to stakeholders, unless they have strong evidence to the contrary, you and your competitors look the same.

This brings me back to the sales process. It is here you have the opportunity to differentiate by building relationships and an unassailable business case that eliminates your competitors as alternatives.

Improve Your Power Position

Because you are negotiating all of the time—sometimes multiple times a day or week—you must *always* be thinking about how you can strengthen your power position. This is sales negotiation game strategy, and it's always on.

Your overriding focus as a sales professional, from the time you wake in the morning, to the time you lay your head down at night, is strengthening your power position within the deals in your pipe.

You may strengthen your power position either by increasing your alternatives or by eliminating and neutralizing the other party's alternatives.

To Increase Your Alternatives:

1. Be fanatical about prospecting and build a strong pipeline full of qualified opportunities. This gives you multiple paths to achieving your sales goals.
2. Avoid negotiating important opportunities in a time crunch— at the end of a month, quarter, or year—when the natural pressure to deliver on sales forecasts removes alternatives. This

means getting control of the sales process and managing the timeline.

3. Front-load your year so that you make your number early. This gives you the alternative to detach and walk away from any deal. Prospect heavily in the fourth quarter to fill the pipe for Q1.

4. Leverage relaxed, assertive confidence to insinuate that you have alternatives. This is essentially an emotional bluff. Remember, though, that there is a big difference between relaxed confidence and arrogance.

To Eliminate or Neutralize the Other Party's Alternatives:

1. Actively target qualified prospects that are in the buying window. Urgency eliminates alternatives.

2. Focus on organizations that are a good fit for your product or service and view you and your company as their best alternative. Need eliminates alternatives.

3. Leverage scarcity and time compression to reduce the viability of alternatives.

4. Win first by compelling the stakeholders to pick you as their vendor of choice. When stakeholders make an explicit or implicit decision for you, it diminishes the value of alternatives.

5. Build advocates and coaches. When you map the stakeholder array and actively work to develop advocates and coaches, it helps you leverage social pressure to neutralize the alternatives being pitched by naysayers.

6. Know your competitors. It's easier to neutralize or eliminate a competitor as an alternative if you have the facts.

7. Give the stakeholders a business case for doing business with you that demonstrates how your solutions will help them achieve their desired business outcomes and tie those projected outcomes to metrics that matter in their business. Building a value bridge to MBOs creates differentiation and diminishes the value of other potential alternatives.

8. Know the numbers—metrics that matter—and be able to use a calculator to demonstrate and make the value bridge tangible.

Get There First—Shaping Operations

One of the most effective ways to eliminate or neutralize the stake-holder group's alternatives is to get there first. Become a fanatical prospector. Begin working with and nurturing prospects far ahead of an open buying window. This allows you to both influence the prospect's buying process on the front end and eliminate competing alternatives.

Getting there first allows you to assume a consultant's role and thus shape buying decisions and your win probability. You have the opportunity to help stakeholders develop the criteria for evaluating vendors and teach them how to buy.

In this shaping role, you have the opportunity to influence and even write RFPs and bid specs. You may lay land mines for competitors and add, subtract, or change steps in the buying process. In doing so, you strengthen your power position by eliminating, weakening, or neutralizing alternatives.

We have helped many of our clients understand the value of getting there first. When their salespeople are engaging prospects ahead of the opening of the official buying window, the closing rates and profitability of their deals soar. For one client, their closing ratio was over 70% when they were proactive and got into the deal early, but their ratio was less than 10% for deals when they were brought in late.

Of course, sometimes you are unable to get in the deal ahead of competitors. This is when you must use leverage to bend the buying process back to your sales process, disrupt your competitors' rhythm, and reshape the game board in your favor.

Leverage the Investment Effect and Consistency Principle to Improve Your Power Position

Vincent Van Gogh once said that "great things are not done by impulse, but by a series of small steps brought together." The sales process is effectively a step-by-step series of micro-commitments.

Effective sales negotiators strengthen their power position by using leverage to compel stakeholders to advance through those steps methodically. Along with helping you in relationship building and discovery, micro-commitments strengthen your power position by activating the human value bias and consistency principle, also known as the investment effect.

Humans value that which costs them more. When you pay a high price for something—money, effort, time, or emotion—it means more to you. When humans are given something for free or gain it with no real effort, there is little emotional connection or value assigned to it—regardless of how valuable that thing might be to another person. Likewise, people place a higher value on things that are scarce than those that are abundant—the scarcity effect.

It is also true that humans have a strong subconscious drive to act, behave, and make decisions consistent with their values and beliefs. To do otherwise triggers painful cognitive dissonance.

Cognitive dissonance is the painful mental stress we feel when we attempt to hold two opposing values in our mind at the same time. When you make a promise to someone and then break that promise, it makes you feel bad. That bad feeling is dissonance.

Each time stakeholders make and follow through on a micro-commitment, they must shift their value and belief system to be consistent with that commitment so as to reduce dissonance.

Micro-commitments are the small steps on the long buying journey. Each commitment makes the price paid grow. Turning back becomes more difficult. Alternatives feel less valuable or relevant.

With each micro-commitment, investment in time, or small effort, stakeholders are compelled (motivated) to act in a way consistent with their commitments. They feel an increased emotional connection to you, place ever-increasing value on the process, and have a greater sense of responsibility to move toward an outcome.

When stakeholders consistently invest *time, emotion,* and *action* (TEA) in the sales and buying process, there is a much higher probability that you will:

- Become the vendor of choice.
- Create a deep emotional connection to you and your company.
- Build a strong and compelling business case.
- Eliminate or neutralize alternatives.

Regular micro-commitments create deal velocity and help you maintain momentum. Each step forward makes the next step easier. Micro-commitments also help you *collect yeses.* These small agreements, along the way, give you leverage to minimize or eliminate alternatives during sales negotiation conversations.

During each conversation with a stakeholder, ask for small commitments. Micro-commitments include the next meeting, access to another stakeholder or leveling up to the executive suite, data and information, invoices, copies of contracts, a competitor's collateral, facility tours, breakfast, lunch, dinner, coffee, or anything that requires them to agree to and carry through on a commitment.

Do not leave sales meetings without nailing down the next step for discovery meetings, demos, facility tours, presentations, additional stakeholder meetings; leveling up to the decision maker; getting data for building a business case; or scheduling the next meeting, proposals, and closing/negotiating meetings.

It is important to understand that as a sales professional, your job is to keep the ball rolling, and you should never expect your prospect to do this for you. Therefore, it pays to follow this simple cardinal rule of sales meetings: *Never leave a sales meeting, whether in person or on the phone, without setting and committing to a firm next step with your stakeholder. Ever!*

Anticipate Alternatives

Master negotiators plan for the other side's alternatives. They make a list of all possible alternatives and rank them—identifying the

BATNA. Then they go about systematically building the case for eliminating those alternatives.

The more you understand the other side's options and which stakeholders may be promoting those options as viable alternatives, the more effective you'll be when building your business case. With this knowledge, you'll be able to eliminate, neutralize, or minimize those alternatives at the negotiation table.

This requires you to take off your rose-colored lenses and rise above your confirmation bias—the tendency for humans to see only what reflects their own beliefs. It requires awareness and even a bit of paranoia.

Begin compiling and ranking the stakeholder alternative list from the moment you engage the prospect. Leave nothing to chance. Consider every possibility that they could see as an alternative to choosing you. Then as you move through the sales process, update and rerank the list—BATNA on top.

Ask provocative questions in conversations to bring potential alternatives to the surface. Recognize that stakeholders won't always be truthful with you. They may tell you they have alternatives when they don't in an effort to strengthen their power position.

COMPILED STAKEHOLDER LIST	STAKEHOLDER ALTERNATIVES	BATNA RANK

Figure 12.2   Build the Stakeholder BATNA List.

Stakeholders may also be delusional. They might believe, for instance, that they can build and maintain their own software program effectively. For this reason, you need to know your product, market trends, costs, your competitors, and the prospect's internal capabilities.

Even if you are unable to eliminate alternatives during the sales process, you may be able to use the information to help the other side to see the downside of the alternative they are trying to use as leverage for concessions.

You must do deep discovery to understand their:

- Real current situation
- Negative implications of doing nothing
- Desired end-state goal
- Measurable business outcomes of their end-state goals
- Metrics that matter

It is in the buyer's best interest to have as many alternatives as possible. It is in your best interest to eliminate as many of those alternatives as possible. Your job in the sales process is to build a case that causes them to reconsider what is and isn't a viable alternative.

Daniel J. Boorstin once said that "The greatest obstacle to discovery is not ignorance. It is the illusion of knowledge." The same can be said of negotiation. The illusion is assuming that your proposal is the only alternative your stakeholders are considering. The root cause of making such a false assumption is skipping or short-cutting steps in the sales process.

Status Quo and Safety Biases and Why No Decision Is Often the BATNA

Here's a blinding flash of the obvious: *humans don't like change.* We actively work to avoid it. We stick to our routines and favorites. We live by the heuristic "If it isn't broke, don't fix it."

Whenever someone suggests that a change might be made, we become anxious, cynical, and rebellious—even if that change is in our favor.

Humans live with an underlying fear that change will make things worse. We are driven to avoid making irreversible decisions. This *status quo bias* is the top reason why stakeholders throw out objections and deals get stalled in the late stages of the sales process.

In his book, *Thinking, Fast and Slow*, Daniel Kahneman, the father of heuristic and cognitive bias research, writes:

> Organisms that placed more urgency on avoiding threats than they did maximizing opportunities were more likely to pass on their genes. So, over time, the prospect of losses has become a more powerful motivator on your behavior than the promise of gains.[2]

When faced with options, we gravitate to the one that is perceived to carry the least risk. This *safety bias* causes your buyer's brain to be more aware of bad things (what could go wrong) than good things (what could go right).

In evolutionary terms, it makes sense. Although you might miss the opportunity for a good thing, such as a free lunch, if you were not paying attention to risk in your environment, you could end up with a very bad thing—*being lunch*.

As humans, we tend to be attracted to safe choices and safe environments. Buyers are worried. "What if we make a change and things go wrong?" They worry that you won't live up to your promises and you'll disrupt their business. They worry that you'll manipulate them. And why shouldn't they? The salespeople who came before you failed them when it mattered most.

Buyers bring this emotional baggage into the buying process, and because humans remember negative events far more vividly than positive ones, stakeholders believe that past negative events will be more likely to happen in the future.

When the safety bias is hitched to the status quo bias, it creates a formidable emotional wall that causes stakeholders to do nothing.

The number-one reason why deals are lost to *no decision* is the fear of negative future consequences.

These pernicious cognitive biases, working in concert, cause your stakeholders to subconsciously magnify every flaw, every risk, and every concern about you and your proposition—the human negativity bias. They feel uncertain, unsure, and afraid. Therefore, they choose staying put and doing nothing (the status quo) over change.

Even in untenable situations, when change is necessary for survival, people will cling to the status quo: "Better the devil you know than the devil you don't."

It's maddening for salespeople when they lead thirsty horses to water but despite pushing, shoving, and cajoling cannot make them drink. Whether you are trying to influence a prospect to change vendors, coax a customer to purchase a new product, appeal to a company to adopt a new system, or challenge a team of stakeholders to transform their business, they will almost always see status quo as their BATNA.

Master sales negotiators help stakeholders move past their status quo bias by allowing them to acclimate to change through priming and micro-commitments.

1. Advancing through a series of micro-commitments—small, low-risk, easy-to-consume steps—prepares stakeholders for change.
2. Priming change is accomplished during discovery through artful questions that allow the stakeholder to talk about the negative implications of doing nothing while visualizing a desired future state.

Trust, however, is the one emotion that breaks the gravitational force of the status quo. Although few decisions are completely free of risk, trust plays a crucial role in reducing fear and minimizing perceived risk for stakeholders. A foundation of trust is built and earned, one brick at a time, as you move through the sales process and demonstrate, through your actions, that you are trustworthy.

13 | Discovery: The Fine Art of Building Your Case

Discovery is the process of building your case and, in turn, trust. It is the most important step in the sales process. It's where 80% or more of your time should be spent. Depending on the complexity of the deal, discovery may last a few minutes or span many months and require meetings with a broad array of stakeholders.

During discovery, you must be patient, strategic, and methodical. The objective is to leverage strategic, artful, and provocative questions to:

- Create self-awareness that causes stakeholders to realize that there is a need to change
- Challenge the status quo and shake stakeholders from their comfort zones
- Help stakeholders see the flaws in and eliminate perceived alternatives

Except for putting the right deals into the pipeline in the first place, nothing else in the sales process has a greater impact on your position at the sales negotiation table than effective discovery.

It's Not Sexy, but It's the Key to Getting Ink

Discovery can be slow, time-consuming, and emotionally challenging. It requires intention, strategy, and planning. You must ask open-ended questions, demonstrate sincere interest, and listen.

It's so much easier to quickly run through a handful of self-serving, closed-ended questions, email over a proposal, and hope for the best than it is to take the time to truly understand what is important to your prospect and their stakeholders. Human-to-human interaction gets replaced with shortcuts and arms-length communication.

One of the primary reasons so many salespeople struggle at the sales negotiation table is that their discovery was weak and inadequate. They have little ammunition with which to defend or support their position. When a buyer counters that they are just the same as their competitors, whose prices are lower, the salesperson is unable to offer anything more than a discount.

Consider Julie, an account executive, who walks into the office of a new prospect, introduces herself, and begins pitching her company and products.

Raymond, the buyer, eventually tires of the pitch and cuts Julie off. "Julie, our current vendor is doing a pretty good job right now, but we are always open to other quotes. Here is a spec sheet of what we are using now. Work something up, send it to me, and then we can talk. I just want you to know, though, that you'll need to get your prices right."

Julie dashes back to her office and puts together a quote. She tells her sales manager, "I've got a great opportunity over at Arc Lawn Industries. I'm talking to the decision maker, and he's super interested! But I need to get aggressive on our pricing to get this one." She gets approval for the steep discounts and emails her quote to Raymond.

Three days later, Julie calls and gets Raymond on the phone. "Raymond, what did you think about my quote?"

"Your prices are much higher than what we are paying now," he responds.

This sets Julie back on her heels and she tries to recover. "We gave you our most aggressive pricing. Understand, though, that our product is much higher quality than you are getting from my competitor and has more features."

"That may be true, but what we are using now is working. Besides, it can't be that different. You are all about the same. If you want a shot at our business, you are going to need to go significantly lower on your pricing."

Because there was no discovery, Julie has little ammunition with which to explain value. She "showed-up-and-threw-up," and as far as Raymond is concerned, there is no difference between her product and her competitor's product other than price.

Julie's choice is difficult: either discount even further, giving away all of her profit and commissions, or walk. Sound familiar? For many salespeople, this is a normal day.

Negotiation Ammunition

If you've ever had a chance to see an iceberg up close, you know how impressively huge they can be. What is hard to fathom, though, is that what you see of the iceberg is only a small portion of the total mass, most of which is hidden below the water's surface.

Stakeholders are much like icebergs, revealing only surface information while keeping their real problems and emotions hidden from view. It is not natural for stakeholders to allow sellers below the surface. Keeping their cards close to the proverbial vest is how they protect and strengthen their power position.

Discovery is a language of questions. Any question you ask is more impactful than anything you will ever say, and anything you think you should be saying is ten times more powerful when delivered in the form of a question. Artfully structured, open-ended questions that are asked in the context of a fluid conversation keep stakeholders engaged and help you get below the surface.

When you treat discovery as a fluid conversation, you disarm your stakeholders, draw them in, lower their emotional walls to get beneath the surface, and gather the information you need to build an unassailable business case that eliminates alternatives.

The more you show genuine interest in what your stakeholders are saying, the more valuable and important they feel. The better they feel, the more they will want to talk. The more they talk, the more connected they will feel to you. As you connect, you gain the right to ask the deeper, more strategic questions that get below the surface and to the information you need.

Artful questions are provocative. Sometimes they are just simple statements with a pause that elicit responses to fill in the silence. They cause the stakeholder to think and become self-aware. Artful questions are organic, building on the conversation naturally. They must match the moment and cannot be scripted.

Strategic questions are well placed in support of the overriding sales strategy and moving to next steps. These questions are outcome focused and three to five moves ahead on the game board.

Empathy, situational awareness, attention control, emotional control, and confidence are the conduits to asking strategic and artful questions that match the moment.

Many deals are won during discovery because a well-placed question creates doubt about potential alternatives: the current vendor, a competitor, another system or process, the belief that it can be done in-house, or doing nothing. Artful questions provoke stakeholders to consider the implications and risks of failing to act.

It is here that the implicit decision to select you and your company as the vendor of choice begins to form.

The SCORE Discovery Framework

Discovery is about building your case—the value of doing business with you—and eliminating alternatives to doing business with you. SCORE is an easy-to-remember acronym for the key discovery points required to build your business case (Figure 13.1):

S = Stakeholder success criteria

C = Criteria for vendor evaluation

O = Desired business outcomes and metrics that matter

R = Real state situation

E = End state vision

The SCORE Discovery Framework is powerful because it keeps you on track *and* allows you to flex to the context of the situation: different industries, different products and services, dif-

S	STAKEHOLDER SUCCESS CRITERIA
C	CRITERIA for VENDOR EVALUATION
O	DESIRED BUSINESS OUTCOMES/MTMs
R	REAL STATE
E	END STATE

Figure 13.1   Leverage the SCORE Discovery Framework to Become a Powerful Negotiator.

ferent cycles, multiple levels of complexity, different stakeholders, and different salespeople. It easily integrates into any sales process model and questioning methodologies like SPIN.

Stakeholder Success Criteria

Good discovery begins with a BASIC stakeholder map (Figure 13.2). As you've learned, stakeholders play different roles in the buying process, and each will have information you need to build your business case.

Most importantly, each stakeholder will have their own personal success criteria, problems they want to solve, and ideas and

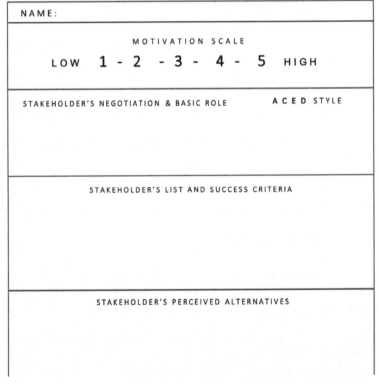

Figure 13.2   Build the Stakeholder Negotiation Profile.

feelings on alternatives to doing business with you. To uncover individual stakeholder criteria, you'll ask questions like these:

- "Tell me what success means to you."
- "Can you tell me about what's most important to you?"
- "What problems are you trying to solve?"
- "What worries you the most about the current situation?"
- "Can you walk me through the alternatives you feel are available to solve these problems?"

You will use the information you learn to build a stakeholder negotiation profile for each individual stakeholder. We'll cover this in more detail in Chapter 25.

Criteria for Vendor Evaluation

It's important that you understand how the stakeholder group and their company will select the vendor of choice.

When you have this information, you'll gain insight on how the company plans to negotiate the deal, how they strengthen and protect their power position, and how to build your strategy to weaken any alternatives by aligning your presentations, recommendations, and business case to the evaluation criteria.

By getting in early, you'll have the opportunity to shape the evaluation criteria with insight and education.

Desired Business Outcomes and Metrics That Matter

Identifying measurable business outcomes (MBOs) and gaining consensus on the value of those outcomes—the metrics that matter (MTM)—is where you earn your chops.

Some of those MBOs will be out in the open and already identified by the stakeholder group. The magic in discovery, though, is bringing problems, pain, and opportunities to the surface through artful and strategic questions.

Effective discovery should help stakeholders become aware of the opportunity to create MBOs that can transform their business. As you make these MBOs feel tangible to the stakeholder group, alternatives to doing business with you begin to fade away and your power position strengthens.

Measurable, though, is the key to making your case at the negotiation table. You must have intimate knowledge of the MTMs. When you are being pressured to lower your prices or unfairly compared to competitors, you can easily flip the script by getting out your calculator and demonstrating the value of your proposal in black and white.

Real State

One alternative that is always on the table is staying put—doing nothing. For this reason, you must dig deep to understand the *real* current state of affairs.

Stakeholders will obfuscate and hide the truth for various reasons, including embarrassment, delusion, disconnection, and attempting to protect the strength of their position. This is why you must spend time with multiple stakeholders, go through a discovery process before demos, tour facilities, spend a day observing how they do business, and dive into the data to get the true story.

Because the status quo and safety biases are always in play and doing nothing is almost always perceived as the strongest alternative, you must make it your mission to eliminate "no decision" as an alternative. You do this by:

1. Asking provocative questions that bring the real state to the surface and make stakeholders aware of the need to change.
2. Helping the stakeholders internalize why the real state is untenable and unsustainable.
3. Leverage amplifiers to push current organizational pain up to the key stakeholders who may be impacted.
4. Leverage information, insight, and the stories you've gathered to engage stakeholders who are disconnected from reality.

End State

The end state, or future state vision, is tied to the business outcomes and stakeholder success criteria. Here you begin to move stakeholders higher on the motivation scale.

The objective is to get stakeholders in all BASIC roles to articulate their vision for the future. This vision will be the focus of your business outcome map, proposal, and value bridges.

14 | Qualifying

If I had a dollar for every time I've heard a sales leader or sales enablement professional exclaim, "We're pretty good at selling; we just don't know how to close," I'd have my own private island.

I understand the frustration of the leaders of these salespeople. It's hard to watch their sales teams struggle and even harder to justify missing sales numbers and forecasts.

Certainly, there are lots of reasons that salespeople fail to get ink:

- Engaging with stakeholders who cannot make decisions
- Failing to ask for and gain micro-commitments that advance the deal
- Pitching features rather than building a relevant business case linked to measurable business outcomes
- Negotiating before being selected as the vendor of choice

These things may all be true, but the brutal truth is when sales-people are having a difficult time closing there is almost always a direct correlation to a pipeline that is stuffed with opportunities that fail to meet even minimum qualification standards.

It's not uncommon for my consultants at Sales Gravy to run murder boarding sessions (see my book *Sales EQ*) on a client's pipeline and kill half to two-thirds of the deals in the pipe. It's an eye-opening and gut-wrenching experience for leaders and their sales professionals to come face to face with the fact that their pipeline is a fabrication. It hurts, but you cannot take delusion to the bank.

When you choose delusion over reality, you are making a conscious choice not only to lie to yourself but to lower your standards and performance. Reality is the realm of the effective sales negotiator, and joining reality is one of the first steps on the road to winning for your team at the sales negotiation table.

Awareness, though, is the mother of change, and this exercise helps them get sales productivity back on track and shift time, resources, and attention to pipeline opportunities that have the highest probability of closing.

Everything Begins with a Qualified Prospect

This is why I need to level with you: Nothing you learn in this book matters a hill of beans if you are not dealing with qualified prospects.

You can be the greatest closer and negotiator the world has ever known, but if you are dealing with prospects that are not in the buying window or stakeholders who are unwilling to engage and make micro-commitments that advance your deal through the pipeline, you will have nothing to negotiate. Period. End of story.

In sales, everything begins with a qualified prospect. Time is money, and it is a waste of time to work with prospects that are not going to buy. A moment spent with a low-probability prospect takes you away from your most important task: investing in deals you can ink.

When you invest in poorly qualified deals—especially when the timing is wrong, there are many alternatives, or you are working with the wrong or unengaged stakeholders—it's easy to default to discounting to entice these losers into signing. In the process you give away leverage, profits, commissions, and your self-respect in the process.

The qualifying journey begins with gathering information while prospecting. It continues during your initial conversations with stakeholders and into discovery, maintaining acute awareness throughout the entire sales process, up to the moment you get ink, for signs that might disqualify or lower the win probability of your deal.

Here's the good news, though. When you are working with qualified companies, stakeholders, and deals, your leverage and power position improve, because your timing will be right, they will be more motivated, and your business case will be relevant to their unique situation and challenges. This gives you the highest probability of closing deals at the highest prices and with the most favorable terms and conditions.

Developing an IQP Profile

Effective qualifying begins with defining your ideal qualified prospect (IQP). This profile is a composite that includes the buying window, compelling buying motivations, stakeholder hierarchies, engagement, competitor entrenchment, sales cycle, industry vertical, company size, and fit, among other attributes. An IQP helps you target, nurture, and engage the right prospects at the right time. Leverage the IQP profile to build targeted prospecting lists and benchmark existing pipeline opportunities.

If you work for a large established company, it's likely that an IQP profile has already been created. This profile will vary based on account size, market vertical, product, or service.

If you work for a small company or a start-up that hasn't developed an IQP profile, begin by analyzing your product and service delivery strengths and weaknesses. Look for patterns and commonalities among your best customers. Define and map common stakeholder roles that are responsible for purchasing what you sell. Analyze the deals you are closing to gain a deeper understanding of the events that trigger the opening of buying windows.

Once you have gathered sufficient information, develop a profile of the prospects most likely to do business with you and become profitable, happy customers. Of course, not every deal will fit your IQP profile perfectly. This is not how the real world works. Most opportunities are imperfect. Qualification is a combination of both data and sales intuition.

You must consider factual evidence and listen to your gut instinct when assessing the viability of a deal. Along the way, you must make a series of decisions to discern if the opportunity merits your continued attention and if you can improve your power position.

Nine-Frame Qualifying Matrix

I'm a fan of simple and visual. One of my favorite tools for developing an IQP profile and managing the ongoing qualifying journey is the nine-frame qualifying matrix affectionately called the 9-BOX. This tool offers a visual representation of data points for qualification across nine frames and six independent dimensions.

I love this tool because it's eye-opening. The 9-BOX makes it very easy to see exactly where you stand in any deal at any point in the sales process. It helps identify gaps in your knowledge, potential deal killers, and weaknesses in your power position.

Some of my clients even use it as scorecard by placing value on the frames and qualifying points to build a composite score of each opportunity. This makes it easier to make data-driven judgments about deal win probability.

See Figure 14.1. You'll notice that there are three columns across the top labeled:

1. TQ—technical qualifiers
2. SQ—stakeholder qualifiers
3. FQ—fit qualifiers

Next, you'll find three rows labeled:

1. HPP—high-potential prospect
2. MPP—medium-potential prospect
3. LPP—low-potential prospect

Note: As I get deeper into the sales process, I substitute the word "potential" for probability, as my focus inside the sales process is improving my power position and bending win probability in my favor.

	TQ	SQ	FQ
HPP			
MPP			
LPP			

Figure 14.1 The Nine-Frame Qualifying Matrix (9-BOX).

Technical Qualifiers

Technical qualifiers (TQs) are quantifiable facts and figures. This is the easiest information to gather before engaging a prospect. For example, at Sales Gravy we sell e-learning solutions through our Sales Gravy University platform.

Target prospects for this service have $5 million to $250 million in revenue, are privately owned, and have 5 to 100 sales resources on the team. These prospects have the highest propensity to purchase self-directed online learning and virtual instructor-led training (VILT) on Sales Gravy University. As we move away from this IQP sweet spot, our win probability recedes.

Stakeholder Qualifiers

This column of the qualification matrix is focused on stakeholders and engagement. Stakeholder qualifiers (SQs) help define the roles and the authority of the people you are dealing with and their level of engagement.

For example, if I'm dealing with an engaged CEO in a complex deal, it's an HPP SQ. On the other hand, if I'm on the receiving end of a blind request for proposal (RFP), I've got an LPP SQ.

Stakeholder qualification is tied directly to mapping the stakeholder array within the opportunity—BASIC. Stakeholder mapping, though, goes beyond the typical focus on identifying the decision maker. It focuses on uncovering the various stakeholders who influence the outcome of a deal, their BASIC role, motivation, and their level of emotional engagement.

Fit Qualifiers

Sometimes you don't fit prospects—their expectations, needs, requirements, demands, buying process, and so on. Sometimes they don't fit you—your unique products and services, capabilities, culture, values, processes, and so on.

Fit is important because the better the fit, the easier it is for you to neutralize the stakeholder group's perceived alternatives.

Your job as a sales professional is to acquire customers that are the best overall fit for both parties. This ensures that your customer gets maximum value while your organization earns maximum profit.

Many salespeople pursue deals that are not a good fit. The consequence of these ill-fated partnerships are unhappy customers who make demands on your business that you cannot fulfill, ultimately costing you money and, at times, your reputation.

Some fit qualifiers may be discerned before you ever meet with a customer. In most cases, though, you'll need to spend time in the discovery stage of the sales process to gain a better understanding of your prospect's current and future requirements, demands, and expectations.

My favorite way to analyze fit is a simple fit matrix (Figure 14.2). This matrix focuses on two dimensions:

1. Fit level
2. Profitability of the account

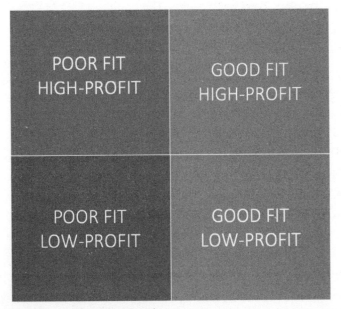

Figure 14.2 The Fit Matrix.

Fit qualifiers include (but are not limited to):

- Value alignment
- Process alignment
- Expectations and demands
- Ease of service delivery
- Willingness to collaborate on solution development
- Value for the expertise you and your company bring to the table
- Timing
- Location

Profitability is usually relatively straightforward but can be negatively impacted by poor fit. For example, if a customer/stakeholder is especially high-maintenance or requires your company to employ nonstandard processes and workflows to service them, it can take a chunk out of the bottom line—sometimes leading to resentment.

It takes pipeline discipline to stay away from accounts that are hard to work with and generate low profits. Salespeople have a bad tendency of engaging and adding poor fit prospects to their pipeline. The primary reason is these prospects are easy to move into the pipeline because no one else wants to work with them.

It is OK to work with a limited number of poor fit but highly profitable customers under the right circumstances. You should only engage in these deals when you have a strong power position that allows you to negotiate very favorable pricing, terms, and conditions.

Ultimately, though, you should be actively targeting prospects in the good fit quadrants. This is the key to maximizing your profits while delivering on your promises and maximizing value for your customers.

Leveraging the Nine-Frame Qualifying Matrix

To use the 9-BOX to develop an IQP profile, fill in each frame with the general attributes of a prospect that might meet that qualification level. For example:

In the HPP/TQ frame you might include:

- Greater than $2 billion in annual revenue
- CIO headquartered in the United States
- Global footprint
- Greater than 10% annual growth rate

In the HPP/SQ frame you might include:

- Direct access to the CIO
- Direct access to the head of security and compliance
- Stakeholder map identified

In the HPP/FQ frame you might include:

- At least one serious data breach in the previous 24 months
- Project team in place
- Budget and funding approved
- Need and value our expertise

The 9-BOX is not static, however. Things change as deals advance through the sales process and as you gather information, map stakeholders, and gain micro-commitments. Some information, like fit qualifiers, may not become clear until you are deeper into the discovery phase of the sales process.

Sometimes opportunities start looking better and win probability improves. Other times the 9-BOX tells the truth—it's time to cut your losses.

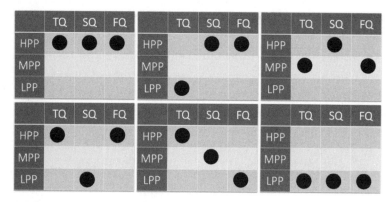

Figure 14.3 Examples of Plotting Ideal Qualified Prospects on the 9-BOX.

When you are using the 9-BOX, it's important to understand that each frame is independent of the other frames (Figure 14.3). Some deals may be HPP/TQ yet MPP/SQ and LPP/FQ.

Sometimes deals line up perfectly in the HPP row, but such unicorns are rare. Most deals are imperfect, and your job is to determine if you should be working on the deal in the first place or if you have the leverage to reshape the game board and improve the viability of the deal.

PART IV

Emotional Discipline

15 | The Seven Disruptive Emotions

Suppose that two emotionless robots were negotiating a deal. How would they would proceed?

The two computers would gather and crunch all the readily available data. Then, out of all the possible outcomes, they would compute the most logical, reasonable, and equitable outcome for both parties.

That's how robots negotiate, and it is how humans *think* they negotiate—on logic and reason. Don't believe me? Just ask them.

But it's not how humans actually negotiate. Robots lead with logic and reason because it's all they have to work with. Humans lead with emotion, because it's how we work. It's simple neuroscience and exactly why humans are so incredibly predictable. We feel, then we think.

Human emotion has a profound impact on each party in the negotiation—even for the people in procurement and purchasing who sometimes act like robots. It adds an infinite set of variables to sales negotiations, which is why very few human-negotiated outcomes are truly logical, reasonable, and equitable.

For you, the sales professional, negotiation can push you to the edge of emotional extremes. Your disruptive emotions are your Achilles' heel in sales negotiations. Unmanaged, they betray you, make you weak, cause you to lose self-control, and put you at a disadvantage with buyers who have been professionally trained to master their emotions when negotiating with salespeople.

Disruptive emotions produce destructive behaviors that fog focus, cloud situational awareness, cause irrational decision making, lead to misjudgments, and erode confidence.

The brutal truth is that in every negotiation, the person who exerts the greatest emotional control has the highest probability of achieving their desired outcomes. To become a master negotiator, you must first learn to master and rise above the disruptive emotions that are holding you back. These seven disruptive emotions impede your ability to negotiate:

- **Fear** is the root cause of most failures in sales. It causes you to hesitate and make excuses rather than confidently and assertively ask for what you want. Fear inhibits prospecting, leveling up to C-level prospects, getting potential objections on the table, moving to the next step, asking for the sale, and negotiating effectively. It clouds objectivity and breeds weakness and insecurity.
- **Desperation** is a disruptive emotion that causes you to become needy and weak, be illogical, and make poor decisions. Desperation makes you instantly unlikeable and unattractive to other people; thereby, it creates a vicious cycle that generates even more rejection. Desperation is the mother of insecurity.
- **Insecurity** drowns confidence and assertiveness. It causes you to feel alone—as if you and only you have a big sign on your back that says "reject me." Insecurity causes you to feel as if rejection is lurking around every corner, so you become gun-shy—afraid of your own shadow.

- **Need for significance** is a core human desire and weakness. Every human being has an insatiable, unfillable need to feel important—to know that they matter and belong. This need to feel important is the singularity of human behavior. Everything we do—good and bad—revolves around this insatiable need. Humans have a compelling need to be accepted and become part of the "in-group." This explains why negotiation is such a powerful emotional destabilizer.

  Negotiation is a form of conflict, with each side focusing on winning for their team. In that moment, you must detach from your need to be accepted. When this need gets out of control, it can become one of our most disruptive emotions—causing irrational behavior. The insatiable need for significance is the mother of attachment and eagerness.

- **Attachment** causes you to become so emotionally focused on winning, getting what you want, looking good in front of others, wanting everyone to agree with you, and always being right that you lose perspective and objectivity. Attachment is the enemy of self-awareness and the genesis of delusion. It creates blind spots at the sales negotiation table that cause you to miss the big picture and paths to compromise and negotiated outcomes.

- **Eagerness** causes you to become so focused on pleasing other people that you abandon your sales negotiation objectives. You falsely believe that "win-win" negotiation means that the buyer must be happy. Eagerness causes you to give in and give up too soon. It is the shortest path to getting taken advantage of at the sales negotiation table.

- **Worry** is the downside of your brain's vigilant crusade to keep you safe and alive. Your brain naturally focuses on the negative—what could go wrong—rather than what could go right. This can trigger a stream of disruptive emotions—based only on your perception that something might go wrong.

Together or individually, these disruptive emotions weaken your position in sales negotiations. Salespeople who cannot regulate disruptive emotions get caught up in and controlled by emotional waves, much like a rudderless ship tossed at sea in a violent storm—pushed from wave to wave, highs and lows, at a whim.

Mastering your emotions is the real secret to mastering sales negotiation. Yet, it is completely disingenuous to tell you that you should just snap your fingers and detach from your emotions. It doesn't work that way. Unless you are an emotionless sociopath, you'll need to deploy sustainable techniques to control your disruptive emotions at the sales negotiation table.

Emotional control in negotiations is a learned behavior. Even buyers who seem to be emotionally detached while pulling concession after concession from you feel some level of discomfort when negotiating. They've just learned to rise above their emotions through awareness, techniques, and practice.

16 | Developing Emotional Self-Control

Emotional discipline is the primary meta-skill of sales negotiation. The combination of situational awareness and the ability to consistently regulate disruptive emotions is at the heart of mastering negotiation, because when you learn how to manage your disruptive emotions, you gain the power to influence the emotions of the other people at the table.

But let's not sweep under the rug just how difficult it is to manage disruptive emotions appropriately in the moment. As humans, we have all been helplessly rocked by waves of out-of-control emotions. We've all said or done things in the moment that in retrospect we regretted. We've all been hit with a hard question at the negotiation table and then stammered and stuttered, searching for the right words in the throes of the fight-or-flight response.

We have all been there, because we are all human. It is easy to talk about managing disruptive emotions in dispassionate clichés, but it is an entirely different thing to quell your emotions in the heat of the moment. Intellect, rational thinking, and process drown in the sea of disruptive emotions and subconscious human instinct.

There Are Only Three Things You Control

When you choose a career in sales, you are choosing a career in which you will be forced to negotiate. There is no way around this.

Because we work in highly competitive markets and sell complex solutions with many variables and pricing models, often with legally binding contracts, negotiation is a norm—not an exception. So, you have a choice. Either give away your commission check and self-respect, or learn to control your emotional responses, gain confidence, and start winning.

You may be able to avoid the emotional discomfort of negotiating in the short term by giving away the kitchen sink just to get deals done. But that has a costly long-term impact on your career, income, and self-esteem.

Getting past the emotions that disrupt confidence at the negotiation table is among the most formidable challenges for sales professionals. It's common to feel intimidated during negotiations with top executives, have diminished confidence when dealing with a tough buyer, or give away valuable concessions out of desperation when you feel that the deal might be slipping from your hands.

It's natural to feel like you have little control when dealing with savvy buyers who have many alternatives and hold your feet to the fire. In these situations, you must focus on what you *can* control rather than what you cannot.

At the sales negotiation table, you control only three things:

1. Your actions
2. Your reactions
3. Your mindset

That's it. Nothing more. You can choose to be disciplined in the sales process. You can choose to be strategic in your efforts to improve your power position. You can choose to plan sales negotiations in advance. You can choose your attitude and self-talk. You can choose awareness over delusion. In emotionally tense situations, you have absolute control over your response.

Self-Awareness

The genesis of much of our behavior—good and bad, destructive and effective—begins outside of the reaches of our conscious minds. We act but are unaware of why we act unless we choose to tune in and become aware. To win at the sales negotiation table, you must maintain a disciplined awareness of your emotions and how they may affect other people.

Mastering your emotions begins with your awareness that the emotion is happening. This allows your rational mind to take the helm, make sense of the emotion, rise above it, and choose your behavior and response.

Awareness is the intentional and deliberate choice to monitor, evaluate, and modulate your emotions so that your emotional responses to the people and environment around you are congruent with your intentions and objectives.

Intentional awareness is the key. Emotions happen without your consent. Therefore, you cannot choose your emotions, only your response.

There is a big difference between experiencing emotions and being caught up in them. Awareness allows you to gain rational control over your emotions and choose your actions appropriately.

Self-awareness opens the door to self-control. Whenever you are buffeted by the emotional storms activated by the conflict of sales negotiation, you simply take control and change course.

Once you become aware that the emotion is happening, self-control allows you to manage your outward behavior despite the volcanic emotions that may be erupting below the surface. This is how you display a relaxed, confident poker face when negotiating. Like a duck on the water, you appear calm and cool on the outside even though you're paddling frantically just below the surface.

Obstacle Immunity

Self-awareness and self-control are like muscles. The more you exercise them, the stronger they get. The best way to exercise them is to face adversity, challenges, and emotional obstacles. In other words, practice.

During World War II, Lawrence Holt, who owned a merchant shipping line in Britain, observed something that launched a movement. His ships were being targeted and torpedoed by German U-boats. Strangely, the survivors of these attacks were more likely to be older sailors than younger, more physically fit men.

This phenomenon led Holt to turn to Kurt Hahn, an educator who before the war had been imprisoned by the Nazis for criticizing Hitler. Holt engaged Hahn to help him understand why the younger, stronger, more physically fit members of his crews died at an alarmingly higher rate after attacks.

What Holt and Hahn eventually concluded was the difference between the two groups came down to emotional resilience, self-reliance, and inner strength. Even though the younger men possessed superior physical strength and agility, it was the emotional resilience to endure grueling obstacles that helped the older, more experienced sailors survive.

Holt is famous for saying, "I would rather entrust the lowering of a lifeboat in mid-Atlantic to a sail-trained octogenarian than to a young sea technician who is completely trained in the modern way but has never been sprayed by saltwater."

The findings led Hahn to found Outward Bound, an organization that, ever since, has been helping people develop mental strength, confidence, tenacity, perseverance, resilience, and obstacle immunity by immersing them in harsh conditions.

Joe De Sena's Spartan Races and military training are designed for the very same purpose—to build obstacle immunity. People are pitted against challenging and painful tests of will. Through adversity and suffering, participants learn how to change their mental state and gain control of disruptive emotions.

You build your "emotional discipline muscle" when you put yourself in a position to experience a perceived obstacle, like negotiation, and the accompanying emotions again and again. But for many people living in Western society, we haven't developed negotiation-specific obstacle immunity because we rarely negotiate.

An easy way to remedy this is to go to flea markets, garage sales, and antique stores for practice. These low-stakes negotiations are the perfect place to tune into self-awareness and practice self-control.

Once you intentionally begin to face your fears and emotionally uncomfortable situations, you'll learn to disrupt and neutralize the anxiety that comes right before the obstacle. You'll begin shifting your internal self-talk and outward physical reaction to rise above the emotion.

Soon negotiation becomes routine. In other words, the more often you negotiate, the more your emotional self-control will improve and the easier it will become. The emotional rigors of sales negotiation will cease to faze you.

Obstacle immunity means having the mental toughness and attention control to reach peak performance while maintaining a positive mindset, no matter when adversity presents itself.

Four Steps to Developing Negotiation Obstacle Immunity

1. Be ready and open to gaining resilience through the crucible of adversity and pain.
2. Intentionally choose to put yourself in uncomfortable situations.
3. Actively seek out the conflict of negotiation by asking for what you want.
4. Push through the desire to go back to your old state of comfort and delusion.

On the other side, you'll gain a sense of mastery and confidence. This leads to higher self-esteem and improved effectiveness at the sales negotiation table.

17 | Relaxed, Assertive Confidence

Nothing improves your leverage and influence at the sales negotiation table more than relaxed, assertive confidence. When you pair relaxed, assertive confidence with sound strategy and excellence throughout the sales process, you bend win probability decidedly in your favor.

One truth about human behavior is that people tend to respond in kind. In other words, emotions are contagious. Humans are very good at picking up on the emotions of other people without much conscious effort.

Because we work and live in groups, we are subconsciously scanning those around us for clues about their emotional state—facial expressions, body language, the tone and inflection of their voice, and the words they use. We then interpret those clues and alter our approach to people based on our perceptions.

This is called *emotional contagion,* and it makes it very easy for humans to both feel what other humans are feeling and transfer emotions to other people. Knowing how to leverage emotional contagion is a powerful meta-skill for influencing human behavior in the sales process and at the negotiation table. When used correctly, it is a powerful form of leverage.

When you approach sales negotiation with relaxed, assertive confidence, stakeholders respond in kind. They lean into you, respond positively, and respect your positions. You gain control of the process, agenda, and pace. Relaxed, assertive confidence gives you leverage to alter the behaviors of stakeholders, making them more willing to:

- Be transparent
- Accept your business case
- Trust your explanations for price positions or terms and conditions
- Comply with your requests
- Offer concessions

Deep Vulnerability

Yet, when you approach the sales negotiation table with relaxed, assertive confidence and maintain that confidence during the negotiation, it means putting it all out there and taking an emotional risk, with no guarantees, no cover, and no place to hide. There is always the chance that your approach will be rebuffed and rejected or that stakeholders will scoff at your business case, balk at your explanations, dismiss the defense of your position, and refuse to negotiate in good faith.

This potential for both conflict and rejection triggers a deep sense of vulnerability causing you to shift your approach to a more passive and defensive stance. This feeling of vulnerability creates a host of disruptive emotions that impede your ability to be effective and strong in sales negotiations.

My wife and I were in a store in North Carolina this past fall, shopping for furniture for our mountain cabin. This was not your typical furniture store, though. All the furniture was handmade by local artisans. Each piece of furniture was unique, and the price of everything was negotiable. I knew this because we'd already scored 20% discounts on several items just by asking.

It was easy. The salesperson didn't hesitate to give us money off our purchases. The funny thing, though, was that the longer we were in the store, the less inclined I was to ask for more discounts. In fact, the last three items we picked up we bought for full price with no attempt to negotiate.

As we drove away, I was kicking myself. I'd left money on the table. Why hadn't I continued asking for more concessions? The honest answer was that it made me feel bad.

I changed my behavior because I wanted to fit in. Not fitting in made me feel vulnerable. I didn't want to push too hard or go too far. I wanted the nice sales rep to like me. It was totally irrational, because the rep was happy to give discounts, and I hadn't even negotiated very hard.

Negotiation is uncomfortable for many people in Western society. Unlike some other cultures, in which haggling over price is a standard part of buying anything, for the most part we don't negotiate. Almost everything we purchase has a list price that we don't question. There are some exceptions, like buying cars. But even the automotive industry is shifting to a no-haggle model because the negotiating process makes buyers feel so uncomfortable.

The truth is that negotiating makes most people feel uncomfortable and vulnerable, which is why we prefer to avoid it. When you are in the heat of a negotiation, when you are on the cusp of asking for what you want, everything in your body and mind screams at you to *stop*. You hesitate because you don't want to be too pushy, cross the line with your assertiveness, or make other people think poorly of you.

Yet, when you give off this insecure vibe, it transfers to the buyer. In your effort to "be more likeable" you can come off as weak and insecure, causing buyers to steamroll you in their attempt to score concessions.

18 | Emotional Contagion: People Respond in Kind

I've spent most of my life around horses. Horses have an innate ability to sense hesitation, insecurity, and fear. A horse tests new riders and takes advantage of them the moment it senses that the person is afraid or lacks confidence.

Horses have a 10-to-1 weight and size advantage over the average person. If the horse doesn't believe that you are in charge, it can and will involuntarily dismount you.

Stakeholders are no different. Your emotions influence their emotions. If they sense fear, weakness, insecurity, or lack of confidence, they will take advantage.

For this reason, when horses or people challenge you, no matter what emotions you are feeling, you must respond with a noncomplementary behavior—a behavior that acts as leverage to counter and disrupt their pattern.

When you lack confidence in yourself, stakeholders tend to lack confidence in you. This is why you must develop and practice techniques for building and demonstrating relaxed confidence and intentional assertiveness even when you feel the opposite. Even if you must fake it because you are shaking in your boots, you must appear relaxed, poised, confident, and in control. You must don your sales negotiation "poker face."

This begins with managing your nonverbal communication to control what the stakeholder sees, hears, and notices subconsciously, including your tone of voice, inflection, pitch, and speed, along with body language and facial expressions. Table 18.1 contrasts the nonverbal communication of an insecure salesperson to that of a relaxed, confident, and assertive salesperson.

Use assertive and assumptive words, phrases, and voice tone, and you will be more powerful and credible when you make your case at the sales negotiation table.

Table 18.1 Nonverbal Communication

Demonstrates Lack of Confidence, Insecurity, and Fear	Demonstrates a Relaxed, Confident Demeanor
Speaking with a high-pitched voice.	Speaking with normal inflection and a deeper pitch.
Speaking fast. Fast talkers seem untrustworthy.	Speaking at a relaxed pace with appropriate pauses.
Tense or defensive tone of voice.	Friendly tone—a smile in your voice and on your face.
Speaking too loudly or too softly.	Appropriate voice modulation with appropriate emotional emphasis on the right words and phrases.
Frail or nervous tone of voice with too many filler words ("ums" and "uhs") and awkward pauses.	Direct, intentional, properly paced tone and speech that gets right to the point.

Demonstrates Lack of Confidence, Insecurity, and Fear	Demonstrates a Relaxed, Confident Demeanor
Lack of eye contact—looking away. Nothing says "I can't be trusted" and "I'm not confident" like poor eye contact.	Direct, appropriate eye contact.
Hands in your pockets.	Hands by your side or out in front of you as you speak. This may feel uncomfortable but makes you look powerful and confident.
Wild gestures or hand motions.	Using hand gestures in a calm and controlled manner.
Touching your face or hair, or putting your fingers in your mouth—clear signs that you are nervous or insecure.	Hands in a power position—by your side or out in front of you in a controlled, nonthreatening manner.
Hunched over, head down, arms crossed.	Straight posture, chin up, shoulders straight and back. This posture will also make you feel more confident.
Shifting back and forth on your feet or rocking your body.	Standing still in a natural power pose.
Stiff posture, tense body language.	Relaxed, natural posture.
Jaw clenched and tense look on face.	Relaxed smile. The smile is a universal nonverbal sign that relays, "I'm friendly and can be trusted."
Weak, limp, sweaty palm handshake.	Firm, confident handshake delivered while making direct eye contact.

Change Your Physiology

Studies on human behavior from virtually every corner of the academic world have proven time and again that we can change how we feel and how other people perceive our emotional state simply by adjusting our physical posture. In other words, your internal emotions and perceptions about those emotions are shaped by your outward physiology.

When you feel insecure or vulnerable, you tend to slump your shoulders, lower your chin, and look at the floor—physical signals of insecurity and emotional weakness. This change in posture makes you appear less confident to others and feel less confident on the inside.

Research by Amy Cuddy of Harvard University demonstrates that "power posing," physically standing in a posture of confidence, even when you don't feel confident, impacts testosterone and cortisol levels in the brain, influencing confidence.[1]

A change in physical posture not only elicits a change in emotions[2] but also triggers a neurophysiological response.[3] We know that the hormones cortisol and testosterone play a significant role in creating a feeling of confidence.

Moms, teachers, and coaches have always known this basic truth. They've been giving us this same advice for years. Keep your chin up. Lift your shoulders. Sit up straight. You'll feel better and look better.

19 | Preparation and Practice

Stressful situations like sales negotiations will trigger disruptive emotions that can derail you. In these situations, you may find it difficult to maintain relaxed, assertive confidence and the "poker face" that comes with it. Your nervousness can create insecurity, causing you to look and act as though you lack confidence. Buyers can read you like a book and will take advantage.

Preparing in advance of sales negotiation conversations is a key to maintaining emotional discipline. Poor sales negotiators wing it. They leave negotiated outcomes to chance and their emotions drifting in the wind.

Effective negotiators build their strategy and plan sales negotiation conversations in advance. For transactional and simple negotiations, they run through their game plan before negotiating. With complex and enterprise-level negotiations, they leverage the Sales Negotiation Planner (see page 196) to murder board the deal and build a sales negotiation strategy. I'll walk you through this process in the next section.

Planning in advance of a sales negotiation allows you to:

- Develop an agenda
- Determine best- and worst-case outcomes
- Develop fallback positions
- Understand the consequences of concessions
- Develop targets and limits
- Prepare to flex to stakeholder communication styles
- Review the list of stakeholders, step into their shoes, and consider their viewpoints
- Anticipate and *practice* for multiple negotiation scenarios

Practicing and running through different scenarios is one of the keys to keeping your emotions in check. Go through the negotiation and role-play scenarios with your manager or team members. Play out all the worst-case scenarios so you are prepared for any eventuality. Practicing is a quick and easy way to build obstacle immunity for a specific situation.

On my team, before we go into a closing meeting or a planned negotiation conversation, we practice together and talk openly about where and how our disruptive emotions might derail us. We agree in advance who will say what, who will answer which questions, and where the lines are drawn on concessions. We develop signals to help us alert each other whenever a disruptive emotion is causing our behavior to run amok.

Preparation calms the mind and builds confidence. You'll find that when you take the time to practice, the actual negotiation seems much easier when you are in it. Your mind is prepared to anticipate disruptive emotions, rise above them, and win for your team.

Know Your Emotional Triggers

There are situations, words, types of people, and circumstances in your sales day that trigger disruptive emotions.

Some emotional triggers, like getting cut off in traffic or being confronted by a rude person, occur without your consent. Others, like allowing yourself to walk into a sales negotiation when you are tired, hungry, or overwhelmed with other issues, are self-inflicted.

In some situations, disruptive emotions are triggered by the way certain people communicate. Buyers who are schooled in negotiation strategies and tactics work hard to trigger frustration, anger, eagerness, and insecurity. They know how to become emotionally detached and thwart your efforts to connect with them emotionally. They are aware that such behavior can make you eager to win their approval by giving away concessions.

When you are aware of the specific emotional triggers that derail you and how and where they happen, it becomes much easier to avoid, plan for, anticipate, and respond to them appropriately. It makes you stronger and more resilient.

While you are planning and practicing, put yourself in these stressful situations. Learn to anticipate triggers and become aware of both your physiological and emotional responses before and at the point of the trigger. With this awareness, you will master the ability to consciously rise above the emotion, maintain your poker face, choose your response, and accomplish your objective.

Positive Visualization and Self-Talk

Getting past the emotions that disrupt confidence is among the most formidable challenges for sales professionals. It's common to feel intimidated when you are meeting with top executives, have diminished confidence when engaging with the professionally trained negotiators in procurement, or become insecure and desperate at the end of the quarter if you are in danger of missing your forecast.

Our greatest failures at the sales negotiation table are often self-inflicted. Your brain is hardwired to anticipate and dwell on worst-case scenarios. When you face an emotionally unpleasant task, it is human nature to begin fabricating negative outcomes in your head. Yet without rational intervention, these internal narratives can lead to self-fulfilling prophesies.

For instance, Rahul expects to be raked over the coals by his buyer during the contract negotiation. He worries that his prices are too high and that he won't have enough concessions to give to his buyer. He sees the buyer becoming angry at him, losing the deal to a competitor, and disappointing his boss when he misses forecast.

This negative visualization causes him to worry and feel insecure. He enters the sales negotiation in this state and gives away 100% of his approved discounts before the buyer even raises a finger. Then, in a last gasp of insecurity, he blurts out that he might be able to get his boss to reduce the price even further.

Had Rahul approached the negotiation with relaxed, assertive confidence, his demeanor alone would have generated a more positive outcome. This is an important reason why planning and running through scenarios is so important to strengthening your confidence and approach.

There is an endless and ongoing stream of chatter inside your head, shaping your emotions and outward actions. Self-talk will either build your confidence or destroy it.

Unlike emotions that are activated without your consent, self-talk is completely within your control. *You* make the choice to think positively or negatively. To build yourself up or tear yourself down. To see a glass half-full or half-empty. To be aware or delusional.

Before going into a closing meeting or negotiation conversation, sit quietly and listen to the conversation in your head—the words you are using, the questions you are asking. Then change those words to support the image of the confident negotiator and closer you want to be and to match how you want to act and how you want to feel. Make an intentional decision to remain tuned in to your inner voice. When it goes negative, stop and change the conversation.

This reason is why elite athletes[1] and elite salespeople employ visualization to pre-program the subconscious brain and change their self-talk. When you visualize success, you teach your mind to act in a way that is congruent with actualizing that success.[2]

Begin by focusing on your breathing. Slow it down. Then in your mind's eye, go step by step through each part of the negotiation—each potential scenario. Focus on how it feels to be confident. Imagine what you will say, what you will ask. Visualize yourself succeeding. Repeat this process again and again until you've trained your mind to manage the disruptive emotions that derail you.

20 | The Ledge Technique

The biology that drives your neurophysiological and emotional responses is powerful. In situations where you actively and intentionally put yourself in a vulnerable position, you feel fear. Your pulse quickens, your breathing gets shallow, and anxiety increases.

The evolutionary forces that trigger a sea of disruptive emotions begin to kick in. The neurophysiological response to the feeling of vulnerability makes it challenging to maintain confidence and composure.

It's difficult to control your attention. It's hard to think. Studies have proven that even your IQ drops when you are in vulnerable situations—a big problem when you need 100% of your intellectual acuity to win for your team at the negotiation table.

In the emotionally fueled atmosphere of sales negotiation, unchecked emotions become your most formidable enemy. When you are engulfed in disruptive emotions, you cannot be effective.

The Curse of Fight or Flight

The human brain, the most complex biological structure on earth, is capable of incredible things. Yet despite its almost infinite complexity, your brain is always focused on one very simple responsibility: protecting you from threats so that you remain alive.

Harvard professor and psychologist Dr. Walter Cannon first coined the term *fight-or-flight response* to describe how the brain responds to threats.[1] In one circumstance, this response can save you from certain death, but in another unleashes a wave of disruptive emotions that derail you when dealing with a tough buyer during a negotiation.

Fight or flight is your autonomic, instinctive response that leads you either to stand your ground and fight or to run away when threatened. In some situations, when your emotions have completely run amok, you may even freeze, like a deer in headlights—a very bad move when negotiating—which will be the exact moment savvy stakeholders plow right over you.

Your brain and body respond to two types of threats:

- **Physical:** Threats to your physical safety or the safety of someone close to you
- **Social:** Threats to your social standing: banishment from the group, looking bad in front of other people, nonacceptance, diminishment, ostracism, and rejection

The fight–or–flight response is insidious because it is a neurophysiological response that circumvents rational thought. It begins in the amygdala—the sensory hub of the brain.

The amygdala (which is housed in the limbic system or emotional center of the brain) interprets the threat from sensory input and alerts the cerebellum (your autonomic brain) of the threat. The cerebellum triggers the release of neurochemicals and hormones into your blood stream to prepare you to either fight or run.

To prepare your body to defend itself, oxygen and glucose-rich blood floods into your muscles. However, since there is only so much to go around, blood is moved from nonessential organs into your muscles.

One of these nonessential areas from which blood is drawn is your neocortex—the rational, logical center of the brain. It turns out that from an evolutionary standpoint, thinking through your options is not an asset when dealing with threats. You need to move quickly to stay alive.

As blood drains from your neocortex, your cognitive capacity degrades to that of a drunken monkey. In the clutches of the fight-or-fight response, you can't think, you struggle for words, and you feel out of control. Your mind reels, palms sweat, stomach tightens, and muscles become tense. Your heart rate accelerates, skin flushes, and pupils dilate. You lose peripheral vision, your blood vessels constrict, and you may begin shaking.

If your response is to fight, you may become defensive, angry, irritated, and verbally attack the stakeholder. You may cut the other person off to argue your point. The resulting argument shuts down the process of working through the opposing points of view and gaining alignment on an agreement.

Should your response be to flee, you become passive and non-assertive when asking for commitments, fold like a cheap lawn chair, and give everything away.

In the fight-or-flight state, without rational intervention you are consumed by disruptive emotions and lose control, which is the most common reason salespeople blow it when negotiating.

The challenge you and every human on earth must contend with is that you have zero control over the fight-or-flight response and its uncomfortable physical manifestations. This does not mean you cannot manage your emotions—just that the neurophysiological fight-or-flight response occurs without your consent.

The Magic Quarter-Second

At the sales negotiation table, you will be pushed to emotional extremes by stakeholders who challenge your positions, diminish the value of your proposal, hit you with hard questions, and make you feel insignificant. They will take illogical positions, make power plays, and say things designed to shake you emotionally. They've been trained to do this because when they do, you are more likely to give concessions.

The secret to gaining control of disruptive emotions in the moment is simply giving your rational brain a chance to catch up and take control so you can rise above these disruptive emotions, regain composure, and choose your response.

In her book, *Emotional Alchemy*, Tara Bennett-Goleman calls this the "magic quarter-second"[2] that allows you to keep the disruptive emotions you feel from becoming emotional reactions you express. In fast-moving, emotionally charged situations, the most effective technique for creating this magic quarter-second is the *ledge technique*.

A ledge may be a statement, acknowledgment, agreement, or question. It can also be a noncomplementary response (relaxed, assertive confidence) that disrupts the stakeholders' patterns and their expectation for how you will respond to their approach. Examples include statements like:

- "That's interesting—can you tell me why this is important to you?"
- "How so?"
- "Would you help me understand?"
- "Interesting—could you walk me through your concern?"
- "Just to be sure I understand your question, could you elaborate a little more?"
- "It sounds like you've been through this before."
- "What else is worrying you about that?"
- "This is exactly why we put _____ in our proposal."

- "That's exactly what I thought you might say."
- "I figured you might say that."
- "A lot of people ask the same question before _____."
- "I get why you might feel that way."
- "That makes sense."

The ledge is a simple but powerful technique for gaining control of your disruptive emotions in the moment. When you get hit with a difficult question, red herring, or a direct challenge from a stakeholder and feel your disruptive emotions kicking in, use the ledge to halt the process and rise above them.

The ledge works because it's a memorized, automatic response that does not require you to think. This is important because as soon as our old friend the fight-or-flight response takes over, cognitive capacity deteriorates.

Instead of stumbling through a nonsensical answer, coming off as defensive, weak, and unknowledgeable, or damaging the relationship with an argument, you simply use the ledge technique with a question or statement that you have prepared in advance. This gives you the milliseconds you need to rise above your emotions and the accompanying neurophysiological response, regain your poise, choose your response, and gain control of the conversation.

21 | Willpower and Emotional Discipline Are Finite

Regulating and managing disruptive emotions is a difficult and ongoing process. As soon as you let your guard down, your emotions tend to take over—especially when you are tired, hungry, or stressed out.

Imagine for a moment that you are in the gym lifting weights. You've got dumbbells in each hand, and you are doing curls. At the beginning of the set—the first two to three reps—it's relatively easy. It feels good. By rep twelve, though, it gets much harder to lift the weights.

It's the same amount of weight each time, but lifting the dumbbell all the way to the top of the curl becomes much more difficult. You grunt as you pull the weight up. You start using your body to help push it the rest of the way. By rep fifteen, you give out. Your arms can no longer lift the weights.

This is called muscle fatigue. And it doesn't matter if you are lifting weights, working in your garden, moving furniture, running, biking, hiking, or climbing, there is a limit to your ability to sustain peak performance in those endeavors.

Managing your emotions is no different, and buyers who are great negotiators know this. They know that your emotional resolve is at its peak at the beginning of a negotiation and begins to dissipate and weaken the longer the negotiation goes on. Good negotiators on the other side of the table drag things out, waste time on tedious details, or agree and then change their mind just to erode your emotional discipline.

Avoid Negotiating When You Are Tired, Hungry, or Emotionally Drained

Just recently we spent 60 days negotiating the terms and conditions of a large consulting contract. Both parties agreed on our fee early in the process, but we still needed to work out specific contractual details over the use of intellectual property.

Our executive sponsor and key decision maker did not have the authority to negotiate the Ts and Cs, which left us working with the company's procurement and legal organizations. Tedious doesn't adequately describe the process we went through to word-smith the legal language to satisfy both of these parties.

After sixty days, the key stakeholder was getting frustrated with the pace of the negotiation. She was pressuring us to find a way to satisfy procurement's draconian requirements.

So, on one hand we were working to keep our customer from losing patience and scrapping the entire project, while on the other dealing with a very challenging procurement organization whose intent was to strip away all of our legal protections.

Finally, we managed a breakthrough with one of the corporate attorneys and negotiated language on which we could both agree. Everyone was excited because we could finally get started.

Procurement promised to send over a new, revised SOW and Master Service Agreement the following day. They did not. Instead, they dragged it out another week. At this point, my team and I were utterly exasperated. We just wanted the negotiation to be over.

When we finally received the updated agreement, we discovered that procurement had reduced our fee for the project. It was a sneaky move designed to take advantage of our discipline fatigue. We had been steadfast in insisting on language that protected our intellectual property. And when months of back and forth had finally produced an agreement, we'd relaxed, let our guard down, and begun preparing for the consulting project.

We were tired of negotiating, tired of the conflict, and ready to get started. Frankly, we were so worn down and so ready to get the agreement signed that we almost missed the change procurement had made. Fortunately, our CFO had her calculator out.

Three members of our team, including the account executive who was set to earn a 20% commission on the deal, argued that we should just concede the price change and sign the contract. Their justification was "It's not that much anyway."

Signing the agreement would have been the easy way out. The ordeal would have been over, our customer would be happy, and our team would be getting to work. The problem was that this price change would set a precedent for all future agreements with the client. It would erode our pricing integrity and teach their procurement team how to play us.

So, as exhausted as we were, we went back and insisted that they put the prices that we already had agreement on back into the agreement. Procurement pressed us to make the concession, but at this point we had the moral high ground, and our equally frustrated stakeholder stepped in and took our side. The deal was finally inked, but it took every ounce of our emotional discipline, resilience, and resolve to pull it off.

Regulating and managing disruptive emotions while negotiating is physically draining. When you are mentally drained, tired, physically exhausted, or hungry, you become a far less effective negotiator. When you find yourself in this state, pause and take a break, sleep on decisions, and when you reach a critical point, bring in another person (as we did with our CFO) to look at the situation objectively and keep you from making poor decisions.

22

The Pipe Is Life: The Real Secret to Emotional Discipline

Sadly, most salespeople spend their time at the feast-or-famine amusement park, riding the desperation roller coaster. Prospecting and top-of-funnel activities are not treated as priorities and receive random and irregular effort at best. These salespeople prospect intensely only when they are at rock-bottom with an empty pipeline.

When salespeople hit the bottom with an empty pipeline, they get up close and personal with the Universal Law of Need. *The more you need the deal, the more you'll give away and sacrifice at the negotiation table to get it. The more you need the deal, the less likely you are to get ink.*

When you are desperate, the probability that you will win for your team plummets. Savvy buyers have been trained to take advantage of salespeople who are needy, desperate, and pathetic.

Fanatical Prospecting

The easiest path to emotional discipline is a pipeline full of quali-fied opportunities. When you don't need to win any particular deal, it is easier to detach emotionally and negotiate as if you don't need that account—because, as they say, there are many other fish in the sea. In a position of abundance, you make better decisions and exude relaxed, assertive confidence.

Fanatical prospectors carry around a pocket full of business cards. They talk up strangers on the phone, in person, on social media, email, and anywhere else they can already had agreement on engage with potential customers. They get moving, take respon-sibility, and own their pipeline. They generate their own leads and—through hard work, determination, and perseverance—their own luck.

Fanatical prospectors get up in the morning and bang the phone. During the day, they knock on doors. Between meetings, they prospect with email and texts. At night, they connect with and engage prospects on social media. Before they quit for the day, they make even more calls. When they are tired, hungry, and fed up with rejection, they still make *one more call.*

Master sales negotiators are acutely aware of the dangers posed by an empty pipeline. The brutal, undeniable truth is a strong position at the sales negotiation table depends on consistent and ongoing prospecting.

A full pipeline equals emotional control and power. When your pipeline is full, the probability is much higher that you'll negotiate for and get the prices, terms, and conditions you deserve. Never, ever forget:

The pipe is life!

PART
V

Sales Negotiation Planning

23 | Be Prepared to Negotiate

Most sales negotiations happen at the speed of light. You are negotiating in the moment, in real time, with little breathing room—face to face, via phone, over video, or by text. You present your proposal; the stakeholders bite, and it's game on.

The stakes, pressure, and pace accelerate further when the clock is ticking and delivery deadlines, budget windows, quota, forecast, qualification for President's Club, and a big commission check are on the line.

Walking into a sales negotiation without planning can quickly put you behind the eight ball if you are facing seasoned buyers trained on how to shake your emotional resolve to get and keep the upper hand.

Awareness Versus Delusion

Objectivity is a big problem for salespeople in the emotionally charged environment of the sales negotiation table. When you've worked so hard to get an opportunity into your pipeline, advance through the steps of the sales process, and reach the negotiating and closing stage, the last thing you want to do is lose it.

Once you've made a significant investment in a deal, it can be a challenge to detach emotionally and approach the negotiation phase of the sales process rationally.

- Confirmation bias, the human tendency to don rose-colored lenses and see only what we want to see, is strong. You may misread the other side, miss key points or clues, or misunderstand the negotiation chess board.
- Optimism can obscure objectivity and create blind spots.
- Overconfidence, your belief that the "deal is in the bag," can lead you to think that the stakeholders will roll over and accept your terms, so there is no need to plan to negotiate.
- Your naturally competitive nature breeds attachment to winning, which can obscure an easy path to getting a deal done, cause you to approach the negotiation with arrogance rather than confidence, or cause you to become confrontational rather than collaborative.

I will continue to repeat what I've said: In every negotiation, the person who exerts the greatest emotional control has the highest probability of walking away with their desired outcome.

Sales negotiation planning helps you rise above disruptive emotions, blind spots, and biases to decide objectively how you will approach the negotiation. It gives you a bird's-eye view of the negotiation game board and the available moves.

Planning Scales to the Deal Size

Every deal is different. With smaller deals that have fewer moving parts, one to two stakeholders, lower long-term risk, and a primary focus on price, it makes little sense to hole up in a war room and build a complex strategic plan. In these situations, it makes much more sense to take time to review your authority and limits informally, set target and limit zones for the negotiated outcome, and plan a simple Give-Take Playlist (GTP).

With more complexity, more stakeholders, and more at risk, sales negotiation planning should be a formal process *before* your final presentation and proposal, contract reviews, and scheduled negotiation meetings.

Ten Elements of Sales Negotiation Planning

There are ten basic elements involved in sales negotiation planning:

1. Authority and nonnegotiables
2. Stakeholder negotiation profiles
3. Stakeholder negotiation list and BATNA analysis
4. Deal qualifiers and fit analysis
5. Motivation and power position assessment
6. Negotiation parameters
7. Business outcome map and the metrics that matter
8. Target zone and limit zone development
9. Negotiation leverage inventory
10. Give-Take Playlist

While you are going through the process, it's critical that you have the discipline to poke holes in your plan, test your assumptions, ask hard questions, and face the truth about your own motivation, leverage, and power position. On your largest opportunities, leverage the perspectives and opinions of other people. Run through different scenarios. Do not allow logic and objectivity to be clouded by emotional attachment, cognitive biases, and delusion.

24 | Authority and Nonnegotiables

The rules of engagement for sales negotiations are different for every company and every sales role. They can even change based on your tenure and the amount of trust you've earned from your leaders. What is likely, though, is you've at least been given some authority to negotiate.

At one company I worked for, we were given a price list for our services. Along with the price schedule, we received set parameters that governed how much we could negotiate until we hit a floor. At that point we were required to get approval from a manager. We were also allowed to negotiate contractual terms and conditions (other than price) inside a set of parameters.

Our commission payout was tied to those concessions. If salespeople negotiated deals at the top of the price list and held firm on terms and conditions like contract length, the payout was big.

Those reps earned many times more than the reps who gave everything away just to get a sale.

Know What You Have the Authority to Negotiate

Before you negotiate, it's vital that you clearly understand what you have the authority to negotiate. Most organizations define where the lines are drawn and where your authority to negotiate begins and ends. Others, though, are less clear. In these cases, you'll need to ask questions so you don't overstep. Table 24.1 helps you organize and list what and where you have the authority to negotiate, what other people have the authority to negotiate, and when you must remain firm on terms and conditions.

Know What Someone Else Has the Authority to Negotiate

Organizations are keen to balance preserving their profits with winning deals and achieving growth. Where your authority to negotiate ends, someone else's usually begins, and where theirs

Table 24.1   Know Your Authority Limits

What You Have the Authority to Negotiate	What Other People on Your Team Have the Authority to Negotiate	Nonnegotiables and Walk-Away Positions

ends, someone else's begins, etc. These checks and balances are in place to ensure that wise decisions are being made in the emotional cauldron of the sales negotiation table.

Savvy sales professionals are aware of where these lines are drawn and who in their organization has the authority to make concessions. For instance, whenever I was working a monster account in deeply competitive situations, I rarely went it alone. I always took my group vice president to the final proposal meeting because when the negotiation began, he had the authority to make a deal and get ink.

Concessions with Conditions

Whenever you are unable to bring someone with you who has the authority to make a deal, you can leverage the *concessions with conditions* tactic. It works like this:

Stakeholder: "Look, I'm good with everything except the automatic annual price increase. We aren't comfortable signing contracts like that."

Salesperson: "So that's it? That's the only thing holding you back?"

Stakeholder: "I think so. Look, our legal department is not going to approve this because we never sign contracts with automatic price increases. If we can find a way around this, I'll sign the agreement."

Salesperson: "This isn't something that I have the authority to remove from the agreement. But I'll tell you want we can do. We can redline the price increase clause so you can sign the agreement. I'll take it back to my boss and present your case. The good news is she is much more likely to approve this change when the agreement is signed."

Once the buyer signs the agreement, the salesperson takes it back to the person who has the authority to approve the concession. Because the agreement is signed, they almost always do. As they say, "a bird in the hand."

The Double-Edged Sword of Negotiation Authority

Negotiation authority is a funny thing. It can be a double-edged sword. I often hear salespeople complaining about not having the authority to negotiate certain items. They believe that it makes them weak in front of buyers.

I explain to them that it is just the opposite. Not having authority gives you strength. It allows you to get on the buyer's side of the table and become their advocate—essentially working together as a team and collaborating to get a deal done.

It also gives you cover when you need to slow things down and gain space to consider your options. This is one of the reasons why I keep my negotiating authority close to the vest.

When there is an easy path to getting a deal done fast, I'll use my authority to make it happen. But when the requested concessions cut deep into profits or my income, I like to defer the authority to negotiate. This gives me time to consider my strategy, get my calculator out, and either find nonmonetary value trades (funny money) that I can leverage to preserve profit or go back to the metrics that matter and build a better value bridge.

Know What Is Nonnegotiable and How to Effectively Articulate Nonnegotiables

Some things are not negotiable. Generally, nonnegotiables are in the terms and conditions—contractual obligations, payment terms, compliance issues. There are usually bottom-line price points you may not go below.

You must be careful with nonnegotiables. They can put you between a rock and a hard place that causes you to replace them with other expensive concessions if you:

- Mistakenly give a concession on a nonnegotiable that you must retract later (which will cost you)
- Insinuate that these things are negotiable (which will cost you)

Therefore, it's helpful to know your nonnegotiables and review them before entering sales negotiations.

People Want What They Cannot Have

What humans want most is the thing they can't have. When buyers find out that an item is nonnegotiable, they want it more. And when they want it, they put maximum pressure on you. This pressure can cause you to stumble in sales negotiations.

If you fail to control your emotions, you'll respond with insecurity or defensiveness. Rather than just stating the truth with relaxed, assertive confidence, your mouth begins running as you attempt to justify your company's nonnegotiable position that you cannot control.

In this state, you don't sound believable, and the buyer pushes harder. Sometimes you try to relieve pressure on yourself by insinuating that you might be able to do something about the nonnegotiable. Trust me, nothing but trouble follows if you go down this dead-end street.

Some contentious nonnegotiable issues come up frequently in sales conversations—delivery lead times, payment terms, minimums, professional services, set-up fees, contractual terms, etc. When you regularly get beat up on these types of things, it is easy to become gun-shy. In an attempt to protect yourself, you apologize for these nonnegotiables early in the sales process, which can trigger objections.

Don't do this. If you bring up nonnegotiables early, you open the door to making a competitor a viable alternative. If you apologize for them or insinuate that you don't agree with the policies, you weaken your position because you create the impression that you don't believe in what you are selling. You'll also be more likely to give away valuable concessions to compensate for the nonnegotiable.

Three Rules for Nonnegotiables

Three rules for nonnegotiables will help you navigate around them in sales negotiations:

- **Don't bring them up.** Leave them off the table unless the buyer brings them up.
- **Never flinch.** Present nonnegotiables with relaxed, assertive confidence, acting as if they are routine and all buyers accept them without question.
- **Message matters.** Explain nonnegotiables in logical, easy-to-understand terms.

The good news is that when you explain nonnegotiables clearly and confidently, most buyers will accept your explanation and move on to greener fields. Take a moment now to list your nonnegotiables (Table 24.2). Then develop an easy-to-understand explanation that you can articulate with authority and confidence at the sales negotiation table.

Table 24.2   Nonnegotiables and The Whys

Nonnegotiable	Explanation

25 | Stakeholder Negotiation Profiles, Negotiation List, BATNA Ranking

Developing a negotiation profile for the stakeholders who will be involved—directly or indirectly—in the sales negotiation is a crucial part of preparing for the conversation.

For each stakeholder, you will analyze:

- Motivation level
- Negotiation role
- ACED buyer persona (see Chapter 28)
- Individual success criteria
- Negotiation list
- Perceived alternatives

NAME:	BASIC ROLE:

MOTIVATION SCALE

LOW **1** - **2** - **3** - **4** - **5** HIGH

STAKEHOLDER'S NEGOTIATION ROLE - **A C E D** STYLE

STAKEHOLDER'S LIST AND SUCCESS CRITERIA

STAKEHOLDER'S PERCEIVED ALTERNATIVES

Figure 25.1   A Negotiation Profile.

Step into their shoes and consider what is important to them.

- Consider how they will approach the negotiation table.
- Identify your advocates—stakeholders who feel that you are their best alternative—and consider how to best leverage them.
- Identify stakeholders who, because they feel there are other alternatives, may be less motivated to work with you, and consider how you might neutralize their influence.

Stakeholder Authority

When dealing with stakeholders, it's impossible to know everything. That doesn't mean that you shouldn't ask or attempt to discern from your conversations with them the level of authority they have in negotiations with you.

Do your best to understand the negotiation authority of each stakeholder on the team and *who will make the final call*. In business-to-business sales, it's not uncommon to deal with a buyer who can say yes to doing business with you, but has little authority to negotiate contractual terms and conditions and ink the agreement. Yes, we always want to be working directly with the buyers who have signing and funding authority. In the real world, though, that's not always possible.

Though stakeholders may not have specific buying authority, they often have influence. Especially when you are dealing with legal and procurement teams, your stakeholder may not have negotiation authority, but they may be able to tell legal and procurement to back off when they are in jeopardy of killing the deal.

Knowing your stakeholder's limits helps you avoid negotiating an outcome with that stakeholder only to have their legal team, boss, or procurement roll it back. Those rollbacks slow the process down and put you in an emotional bind because you'll be required to fight for the same ground twice.

When a stakeholder doesn't have the authority to negotiate a specific outcome, it's better to take a step back and use your leverage to get the parties who have that authority on the phone or in the room.

If you are about to give a valuable concession to close the deal and get ink, that concession is your leverage. Hold the concession until you have everyone with authority "in the room," so that a final decision can be made, and you can lock in the agreement.

Stakeholder List and BATNA Ranking

Once you've built the individual stakeholder negotiation profiles, you'll compile a consolidated list of the core stakeholder success criteria, desires, needs, must-haves, deal-breakers, and core motivations

COMPILED STAKEHOLDER LIST	STAKEHOLDER ALTERNATIVES	BATNA RANK

Figure 25.2   A Stakeholder List and BATNA Ranking.

(Figure 25.2). Then list and rank all perceived alternatives and identify the other side's BATNA.

Use this information to analyze the collective motivation and position strength of the stakeholder group. This process helps you compare the stakeholder list to your list so you can find common ground with your stakeholders, develop your give-take playlist, and build your strategy for neutralizing alternatives and improving your power position.

Motivation, Power Position, Qualifier Analysis, and Parameters

You've learned that the party with the higher level of motivation to get a deal done is more willing to give concessions to achieve that goal. You've learned that power at the negotiation table is directly correlated to the number of alternatives a party has.

Motivation is derived from emotions and desire. Motivation typically has an inverse correlation to power. The collective motivation of the stakeholder group may be leveraged to reduce the viability of perceived alternatives.

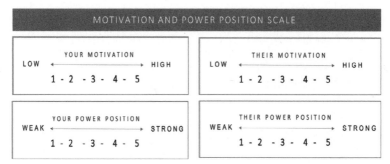

Figure 25.3 The Motivation and Power Position Scale.

Because motivation and power have the greatest influence on negotiated outcomes, it's important to analyze the stakeholder group's motivation and power position collectively (Figure 25.3). Knowing exactly where you stand will help you develop your strategy and approach to the sales negotiation table.

In turn, you must wipe away the cloud of delusion and gain clarity on your level of motivation and your actual power position. This helps you achieve emotional discipline at the table.

One way to do this is to make a quick assessment of the opportunity. Go back to the nine-frame qualifying matrix and map the deal qualifiers. Then run a fit qualifier analysis to determine where the deal fits (Figure 25.4):

- Good fit, high-profit
- Good fit, low-profit
- Poor fit, high-profit
- Poor fit, low-profit

Based on your analysis, determine:

1. How bad do you want this deal?
2. How much are you willing to concede to get the deal done?
3. What are your alternatives if you feel the need to walk away?

Compare the buyer's position to your position. Identify areas where you share common ground. Think about how you might

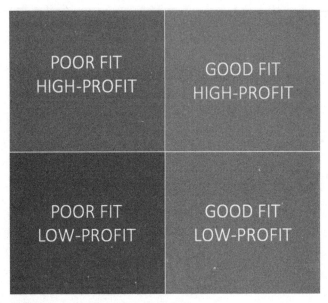

Figure 25.4 Fit Qualifier Analysis.

leverage relationships, information, insights, or concessions to neutralize alternatives and strengthen your position. This process will help you develop target and limit zones for the negotiation and your Give-Take Playlist.

26 | Developing Your Give–Take Playlist

You'll use leverage in the back and forth of negotiating to get alignment with the buyer. When the other side asks for a concession—your leverage—you will ask for something back.

For example, if the buyer asks you to lower your service delivery charge by 10%, you may agree to do so in exchange for an extra year on the service agreement.

It's a simple value exchange. If you give leverage away, it should be paid for with something of equal or greater value. Your overriding goal is to give away things that have a low value to you but a high value to the other side while taking concessions that are of high-value to the other side.

You should never go into a sales negotiation without a plan for how to run these give-take plays. Without a plan, you may give a concession that is valuable to you and get something back that is less valuable to the buyer. Or worse, you may give a concession that is valuable to you but not to the other side, thus neutralizing the impact of the concession.

Sales Negotiation Parameter Analysis

This first step in building your Give-Take Playlist (GTP) is to assess how each party views the five core parameters of a sales negotiation. Leverage the information you gathered during the discovery phase of the sales process on your prospect's criteria for vendor evaluation as a resource for this analysis (Figure 26.1).

1. **Risk.** How much negative risk does each party face by consummating the deal? It is important for you to understand this, because the party that perceives the highest risk will value things that neutralize that risk.
2. **Value.** In light of each party's unique situation, how important is the deal on their value scale? For example, if you are working with a small company, for the owner of that company, your software may be the biggest investment they've ever made. To you, though, it may be a drop in the bucket. Or in reverse, a deal might be a game-changer for you but a routine transaction for the Fortune 100 company you are negotiating with. Understanding relative value is critical for both controlling your emotions and leveraging information and metrics to influence the behaviors of the other party.
3. **Pricing.** It's important to understand how each party views pricing and which price points matter most. You'll want to know whether price or terms and conditions carry more weight:
   - Where is your profit made, and which price points must be protected?
   - Will the buyer fixate on unit price, total price, or total cost of ownership?
   - What is the other side's budget, and is that budget flexible or inflexible?
   - How does the negotiated price impact risk, service delivery, and long-term customer retention?

NEGOTIATION PARAMETERS									
YOUR NEGOTIATION PARAMETERS	LOW	MEDIUM	HIGH	CRITICAL	THEIR NEGOTIATION PARAMETERS	LOW	MEDIUM	HIGH	CRITICAL
RISK PROFILE					RISK PROFILE				
VALUE					VALUE				
PRICING/ECONOMICS					PRICING/ECONOMICS				
TERMS & CONDITIONS					TERMS & CONDITIONS				
RELATIONSHIP					RELATIONSHIP				

Figure 26.1 Negotiation Parameters Analysis.

4. **Terms and Conditions.** In high-risk, enterprise-level deals, terms and conditions matter. You'll want to know which Ts and Cs carry the most weight and to what extent, what your nonnegotiables are, and how they may conflict with the other side's negotiation list.
5. **Relationship.** You will want to gain clarity on the lifetime value of the prospective customer. This helps you avoid digging in on minor issues where you will win a tactical battle only to lose the strategic war. You'll also want to assess how the other side views their partnership with you. Do they value you, or will they defect to the next salesperson who comes along and offers them a lower price?

The sales negotiation parameter analysis is very helpful for scenario planning and preparing for sales negotiation conversations. It gives you insight into the other party's motivation level and power position—especially how they view the alternative of doing nothing.

Business Outcome Map and the Metrics That Matter

The next step in building your give-take playlist is revisiting the prospect's business challenges along with your recommendations and the planned business outcomes from your proposal (Figure 26.2).

Once the stakeholder group has selected you as their VOC, it is safe to assume that they believe your recommendations will help

BUSINESS OUTCOME MAP & METRICS THAT MATTER			
CHALLENGE	RECOMMENDATION	ASSOCIATED BUSINESS OUTCOMES	METRICS-THAT-MATTER (MTM)
1			
2			
3			
4			
5			

Figure 26.2   Check the Prospect's Challenges and Your Recommendations on the Business Outcomes Map.

them achieve those business outcomes. In other words, they saw the value—at least in the moment.

The problem you'll sometimes face at the negotiation table, though, is that they will forget or have a difficult time connecting the value you presented to the price they'll need to pay to realize those business outcomes. Therefore, you'll need to remind them.

You need to be sure that you are prepared to clearly articulate and explain the value you are delivering in the form of measurable business outcomes. The most effective way to do this is with math.

Before walking into a sales negotiation, get your calculator out, and using the metrics that matter to the stakeholder group, prepare yourself to show them, in black-and-white numbers, exactly how they derive value from your offering. Your ability to clearly articulate these value bridges is a key to maintaining contractual and price integrity and avoiding discounting.

Sales Negotiation Map

The starting point in the sales negotiation is your proposal—the formal offer to buy. Frankly, if you've been perfect all the way through the sales process and effectively demonstrated value, you may only need to answer a few questions or deal with benign objections to get ink. That's the best-case scenario: *no negotiation.*

You can't and won't always get what you want, but it doesn't mean that you shouldn't try. You should always approach the proposal phase with the confident assumption that the buyer will say yes to your proposal without negotiating.

Still, it pays to ground yourself in reality. For this reason, you should develop a target and limit zone to guide your give-and-take fallback positions should you need to negotiate. This is your Sales Negotiation Map (SNM; Figure 26.3).

The target zone is a fallback position from your original proposal that still represents a win for your team. It is a negotiated outcome that protects profit, your income, and your organization's ability to deliver on your promises.

The limit is the absolute bottom line for getting a deal done. Beyond that, you bump into nonnegotiables and will be forced to walk away.

Your target and limit zones will be heavily influenced by your motivation to close the deal. Use the qualification assessments—9-BOX and the fit matrix—to guide you in developing the SNM for each deal.

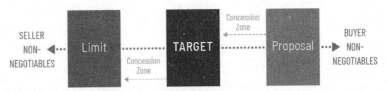

Figure 26.3 The Sales Negotiation Map.

Sales Negotiation Leverage Inventory

Concessions are your negotiation leverage—the value you trade at the sales negotiation table for buyer concessions. These trade-offs are the path to achieving alignment and closing the sale.

Concessions may be high-value trades that impact commissions and profit or low-value, funny money trades that cost little or nothing. Your goal at the negotiation table is to leverage concessions that cost you little in order to protect your income, profits, terms, and conditions.

Begin by building a complete inventory of every potential concession you have at your disposal (see Table 26.1). Brainstorm everything that you can use as leverage in the negotiation. It doesn't matter how small or insignificant the potential concession seems to you; everything has value to someone.

Next, calculate the direct impact of each concession on your income, bonuses, qualification for spiffs, trips, President's Club, etc. Pay close attention to how combinations of concessions change the commission curve. Make a note of which concessions are valuable to you personally and which ones you can give away with little impact.

Then consider the negative impact of concessions on company profits, lifetime value of the customer, other people on your team,

Table 26.1   Concession Calculation

Concession Inventory	Commission and Profit Impact

service delivery, promised solutions, and business outcomes. Consider the unintended consequences of each concession.

Value Is in the Eye of the Beholder

After you've developed a concessions inventory and understand the consequences of those concessions, it becomes easier to develop a concession leverage strategy before each unique sales negotiation by focusing on what the buyer values.

Remember your goal at the negotiation table: *Leverage concessions that are of low value to you but have a high value to the buyer to extract concessions from the buyer that are of high value to you and will compel them to stop negotiating and ink the deal.*

To gain clarity on what is of high value to the other side, begin with the negotiation parameters analysis. Then review the stakeholder negotiation list, stakeholder success criteria, business outcome map, and the prospect's criteria for vendor evaluation.

With this information in hand, develop a negotiation leverage Value inventory (Figure 26.4) that will be relevant in this unique situation. Then gauge the relative value of each leverage point to you and the buyer.

Look for opportunities to leverage funny money. Funny money is any nonmonetary concession that feels valuable to the other side but costs you little.

An example might be video-based training that you offer as part of the package. This carries very little cost to you and your company. During the sales process, though, several stakeholders indicated that this was very important to them because they wanted to use it to drive adoption in their company.

When the stakeholders ask for a concession on price, you can say that you will agree but it will mean that you can't throw the training in for free. When the stakeholders balk at giving up the training, you have leverage to align on an agreement.

NEGOTIATING LEVERAGE	VALUE TO YOU		VALUE TO STAKEHOLDERS	
	HIGH	LOW	HIGH	LOW

Figure 26.4   Negotiation Leverage Value Inventory.

Give–Take Playlist

Now that you have an inventory of concessions and have gauged the value of each concession to you and the other side, the next step is to develop your Give-Take Playlist (GTP; Figure 26.5). The GTP is your fallback game plan for negotiating from your original proposal to your target zone or, if required, your limit zone.

As you develop your GTP, consider how you will use relevant concessions either alone or in combination to align with the stakeholder list and negotiation parameters. Consider how you may need to use certain concessions to neutralize perceived alternatives. Focus on developing GTP items that create a path to alignment on a negotiated agreement that is a win for your team.

Your GTP helps you gain alignment by giving concessions that have a low value to you but a high value to your buyer while taking concessions that have a high value to you from your buyer. Generally, once you reach a point when the buyer is no longer willing to trade concessions, you can then align on an agreement and get ink.

Building your GTP is linked directly to the development of your Sales Negotiation Map. It begins with answering five questions:

1. What do you want—your desired outcome?
2. What is the best-case outcome and the worst acceptable outcome for you and your team?

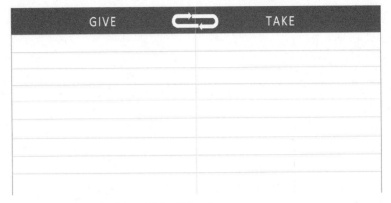

Figure 26.5   A Give-Take Playlist.

3. What are you willing to give up, give away, or sacrifice to get the deal done?
4. What are your absolute bottom-line limits for each negotiable item in the deal?
5. What are the nonnegotiables?

Building your GTP requires you to consider different scenarios. It's akin to visualizing a chess game in your head. Walk through the moves that you anticipate your opponent making. Consider your counter-moves and the unintended consequences of each countermove.

I find it helpful to begin with setting up multiple scenarios based on the opening gambits available to the buyer. For example, the buyer might open with:

- "We love your proposal. Where do we sign?"
- "The price is too high; I'm willing to pay $50,000."
- "We don't want to sign a five-year agreement."
- "We need you to lower the unit rate on widget x to meet what we are already paying your competitor for the same thing."
- "The set-up fees are too much."
- "We don't like the automatic renewal clause in your contract."
- "We can't wait until February for installation; we need this done in the next thirty days."

Then I rank those opening moves based on probability and build my GTP for the ones that are most likely to happen. It's a simple "if-then" process:

- If the buyer asks me to reduce the per-seat subscription cost, I will concede $7.79 per seat in exchange for a *guarantee* of fifty seats.
- If the buyer won't make the guarantee, I will concede $5.25 per seat if they agree to annual rather than monthly billing.
- If the buyer asks for less than a five-year agreement, I will agree to a three- or four-year agreement in exchange for taking back the free training program I offered in my proposal.
- If the buyer asks for no annual price increase, I will agree in exchange for an extra year on their contractual agreement.

GTP planning is fundamental to improving emotional discipline and extracting more favorable outcomes at the sales negotiation table. Going through this process helps you prepare yourself mentally for the give-and-take of the negotiation table during the alignment process.

You'll find that just going through this exercise gets you better connected to the stakeholder group's negotiation list and what is really important to them. It helps you step into their shoes and consider which of your "take-aways" will have the greatest leverage. Finally, it helps you plan for small incremental moves rather than large concessions that deplete your negotiation leverage and leave you in a position of weakness.

Leveraging the Sales Negotiation Planner for Murder Boarding

One of the best sales managers I ever worked for played a game with every big deal in our pipeline called Murder Boarding. We'd get in a room and explore each potential scenario that could push us to our limit zone in a sales negotiation or kill the deal altogether.

This wasn't a broad, 30,000-foot conversation. We dove into the minutiae. Nothing was sacred. All stakeholders, concessions, unintended consequences, potential unknowns, competitors, and our own MLP weaknesses were possible villains.

The sessions, usually conducted with several of my peers, were painful and, at times, embarrassing. Murder boarding exposed blind spots, overconfidence, holes in our value bridges, confirmation biases, and gaps in our knowledge.

- It was uncomfortable to learn that you didn't know important information because you had been too afraid (disruptive emotion) to ask hard questions.
- It hurt to be shaken into awareness that you were unprepared.
- There was pain in coming face-to-face with the fact that you were negotiating too early—before being selected as the VOC.
- It was sometimes hard to accept the fact that you were planning to concede much more than you needed in order to seal the deal.
- It was embarrassing when, as you attempted to explain your position, you got hit in the forehead with a hard "so what?"

Murder boarding pipeline opportunities was uncomfortable. It was also eye-opening. I loved the process because I walked out of those sessions with a better plan that made me much more effective at the negotiation table. I closed many, many deals—on my terms—that would have been lost or landed in my limit zone if not for the insight I gained from murder boarding.

The Sales Negotiation Planner

To help you with sales negotiation planning, strategy, and murder boarding, we've developed and perfected a proven sales negotiation planner. The planner brings together all the core elements of sales negotiation planning we've discussed in the previous chapters.

We offer two formats: an individual planner and a large poster format for team murder boarding exercises.

- You may download a free planner and instructions for your individual use at https://free.salesgravy.com/snp
- You may purchase full-color professionally printed Sales Negotiation Planners (handouts and poster versions) in bulk, including instructions, for your sales team here: https://planners.salesgravy.com

Benjamin Franklin once said that by failing to prepare, you are preparing to fail. This is sage advice for sales negotiation. As you enter the sales negotiation conversation, a well-thought-through sales negotiation plan gives you strength, confidence, an advantage at the table, and a much higher win probability.

PART
VI

Sales Negotiation
Communication

27 | Seven Rules of Effective Sales Negotiation Communication

No matter if your sales negotiation table is an actual table, a phone, video call, email, or text message, it is human-to-human communication and intentional controlled conflict, woven into the imperfect fabric of human emotion and logic.

At the table, effective communication keeps you in control of the conversation so you can move toward alignment on an agreement.

Communication mistakes slow the process down, open the door to alternatives, damage relationships, and lead to costly misunderstandings.

There are seven rules for effective sales negotiation communication that will help you avoid these mistakes. These rules are always in play, and heeding them will give you an advantage in sales negotiation conversations.

To Control the Conversation, You Must First Control Your Emotions

You've learned that emotional discipline is at the heart of effective sales negotiation. Control of the conversation begins with control of your emotions. This is why planning in advance and running through scenarios are so important. The process of planning prepares you to rise above your emotions.

People Respond in Kind

You've learned that emotions are contagious. Because of this, people tend to respond in kind to other people's behaviors.

At the negotiation table, buyers deploy tactics designed to shake you emotionally. They may be direct, bullying, demanding, and pushy. They may be complimentary and sugar-sweet. Their goal is to leverage emotional contagion to get you to respond to them in kind and change your behavior. When you do, they gain control.

On the other hand, when you get people to respond in kind to you, you control the tone, pace, and structure of the conversation. The key to getting people to move toward you and respond in kind is leveraging noncomplementary behaviors. In other words, respond in a way that is the opposite of what they expect from you.

For instance, if they attempt to get you to speed up, slow down. If they attack you, lean back in your seat and respond in a polite and kind manner.

The most powerful noncomplementary behavior is relaxed, assertive confidence. When you are in this state, people tend to respond in kind, lean in, and respect you.

Questions Control the Conversation Flow

Most salespeople believe that to control the conversation, they must do all the talking. I assure you that it is just the opposite. It is the person asking the questions who has control.

When you are asking questions, you control the shape of the conversation and can move it in any direction you please. This helps you keep the conversation on track and focused on your agenda, while also making the stakeholder feel listened to and important.

Always remember that a question you ask is more important than anything you will ever say.

To Know What Other People Are Thinking, They Must Tell You

Learn to listen without jumping to conclusions or making snap judgments. Remember that the speaker is using language to represent their thoughts and feelings. Don't assume that you know what those thoughts and feelings are and finish their sentences.

When your stakeholder slows down or tries to gather their thoughts to find a way to express their feelings or ideas, it is easy to become impatient, jump in, and finish their sentences for them. More often than not, you end up way off base, because you had no idea what they were actually thinking. At the emotionally charged negotiation table, this behavior can create animosity, shut the other person down, and impede understanding.

Humans have a bad habit of assuming that they know what other people are thinking. Do not confuse communication with agreement. The only way to know exactly what someone is thinking is for them to tell you. The words must cross their lips.

When you are unclear about what your stakeholder is saying or if you don't understand something they are trying to express, stop and clarify. Well-timed clarifying questions show the other person that you are listening and are interested in understanding them.

Communication Fails If the Other Party Isn't Thinking the Same Thing You Are Thinking

Back when I was in fourth grade, my teacher, Ms. Gibbons, took the entire class outside on a warm spring day. She lined us all up, about twenty-five kids, and on one end of the line whispered a message that she read from an index card into the ear of the first child. That child then turned to the next person in line and whispered the same message. The process continued as each fourth grader whispered the message to the next person in line until we reached the end.

Ms. Gibbons then had the last child repeat the message out loud to all the other children. There were giggles and snickers. We were all shaking our heads. The words that came out of the last child's mouth were not the words we had passed on.

Finally, Ms. Gibbons read from the index card. The words she spoke were foreign to almost everyone except the first few people in line. Over the course of twenty-five repetitions, the message had become so confused and convoluted that it no longer resembled the original.

I can clearly remember how shocked I was. This demonstration of how poorly we listen was powerful. I think about it each time I encounter a breakdown in communication, which is almost always caused by a breakdown in *listening*.

If you and the buyer are not thinking the same thing, you don't have alignment, and communication fails. Don't assume. Stop, check, clarify, and confirm agreements.

Communication Fails If the Other Party Is Thinking About Your Behavior Rather Than the Deal

At the emotionally charged sales negotiation table, you may be nervous. You'll likely be under pressure to get a deal done. You'll be stressed and worried. You'll want to win.

At these emotional extremes, humans often break from their normal behavior patterns and do things that damage relationships. It's easy to:

- Get into arguments or say hurtful things
- Become rude or disrespectful
- Display arrogance
- Get angry
- Get nervous and come off as less than knowledgeable, weak, or untrustworthy
- Talk over other people and cut them off in your exuberance to explain your position
- Make promises you can't keep
- Fail to listen
- Exaggerate
- Manipulate
- Lie

When your behavior becomes the center of the buyer's attention, aligning on an agreement becomes difficult because they are thinking about you rather than the deal. This is a key reason why emotional discipline is so vital for effective negotiation.

Whenever you get pushed to the brink by a buyer and feel the flight-or-fight response kicking on, pause for a break to collect your thoughts. Otherwise, your disruptive emotions may derail you and your deal.

Do Not Allow Silence to Intimidate You

Silence is one of the most powerful forms of leverage at the sales negotiation table. It compels people answer questions, put issues on the table, object, and commit.

When there is silence at the negotiation table, someone will usually fill in the space with words because it is awkward and intimidating. Those words offer clues to or even reveal the cards the person is holding.

It always amazes me to watch a salesperson make a concession, and then, in the split second of silence while the stakeholder is thinking about it, the salesperson fills in the space with yet another concession.

To remain in control, you must not allow silence to intimidate you. Never answer your own questions. Do not fill in the space. Control your emotions and bite your tongue. Wait for the other person to respond.

28

ACED: Navigating the Four Primary Stakeholder Communication Styles

We each have a preferred style of communicating. Some people are direct, whereas others beat around the bush. Some people speak slowly and exhibit little emotion, whereas others are more animated. People may be direct and driven, analytical and careful, focused on building consensus, or social and outgoing.

You build deeper emotional connections and gain more concessions when you interact with stakeholders based on how they prefer to communicate. Stakeholders tend to like, be attracted to, and be more trusting of people who are like them. This is known as the similarity bias.

Therefore, when you flex your preferred communication style to complement that of the other person, that person will be more open to working with you to align on an agreement.

Flexing your style essentially means adjusting your approach and interpersonal behaviors for each individual so that they are more comfortable working with you, thus easing their anxieties and opening the door for an emotional connection.

ACED

There are four predominant communication styles (Figure 28.1). Labels for these styles shift from psychometric test to psychometric test and from training program to training program. Regardless of the labels, though, the style markers across the multiple theories of human behavior and innate communication preferences tend to converge on these four dominant styles: Analyzer, Consensus Builder, Energizer, and Director (ACED).

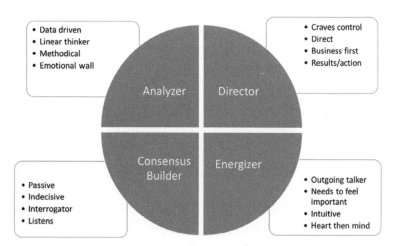

Figure 28.1   ACED Stakeholder Communication Style Inventory.

It is fairly easy to know what style you are dealing with by simply tuning into and observing the other person's behavior patterns. In business, generally, but not always, people tend to congregate in career roles based on style preference. For example, CFOs will be **A**nalyzers, human resources professionals will be **C**onsensus Builders, sales professionals are typically **E**nergizers, and CEOs (and other P&L owners) will often be **D**irectors.

Rarely do people approach the world and the environment around them with a single dominant style. Instead, we are a composite of multiple styles, with a dominant style emerging in stressful or emotional situations—like sales negotiations—when important decisions need to be made.

Analyzer

Analyzers are typically in the role of funding buyers and serve as a check and balance to Energizers and Directors, who are often deal signers. In influencer roles, they can be naysayers who pick your business case apart.

Analyzers are systematic and methodical. They reject hype and pitching, preferring to focus on data and facts. They respond best to linear communication and ironclad case studies. They can often come off as cold and unengaged. Because they easily detach from emotions, they are formidable at the negotiation table.

Analyzers enter negotiation conversations with their emotional walls up. The key to breaking through is methodical patience, controlling your disruptive emotional need to be accepted, and knowing the numbers.

With Analyzers, trust is built slowly. A series of short meetings designed to systematically build the relationship is the best strategy for breaking through.

Begin conversations by asking the Analyzer the most important part of the decision-making process for them. Stay away from personal questions unless they bring the topic up. Instead, focus on business. Ask them about the process they use to evaluate vendors like you. Ask them about their values.

Before negotiating with Analyzers, it is essential that you over-prepare. Consider every question they may ask and ensure you can answer cogently and back your answers up with facts and figures. Do not attempt to BS an Analyzer.

Double-check all written documents, charts, and spreadsheets for typos, inconsistencies, and errors. Analyzers are sticklers for accuracy. They will fixate on inaccurate information, mistakes, or poorly organized data, becoming unable to hear anything else.

To the Analyzer, if you cannot answer questions, back up propositions with facts, or get it right the first time, you are untrustworthy, which eliminates you as a viable vendor or worthy opponent.

Consensus Builder

Consensus Builders value pleasing people and having their ducks in a row. They tend to be predictable, friendly, and good listeners.

Consensus Builders prefer routine and avoid risk and change. They abhor conflict and tend to be passive-aggressive rather than direct when they have issues with other people. Should you offend a Consensus Builder, they will rarely tell you; instead, they will hold a grudge and become resentful. You'll lose the deal and never know why.

Consensus Builders move at a steady and often slow pace. Because they want to be sure everyone feels included in decisions, they take great pains to involve and check with other people. They often ask to see more—another demo, more data, additional case studies, another presentation—earning them the nickname *SeeMores*.

Because Consensus Builders are risk-averse and need all their ducks in a row before taking action, they can be frustrating at the negotiation table. Just when you believe you are on the cusp of inking the deal, they ask for more time to consider your offer and to meet with their team.

If you become impatient and push too hard, you will shut them down. Because Consensus Builders are conflict adverse, once they are shut down, it is very difficult to get them to reengage.

Consensus Builders are great listeners and masters at getting you to talk. They make you feel important and appreciated. They'll interrogate you with questions and allow you to talk your heart out.

After meetings with Consensus Builders, you'll walk out feeling good because you spent so much time talking. Sadly, though, you revealed your hand in the process and gave all your leverage away.

When negotiating with consensus builders, you must be very careful to slow down and earn their trust. Take time up front to gain agreement on exactly what they need to see, hear, feel, and know to make their decision. Gain consensus on a timeline and the negotiating steps.

Meeting with all the people they wish to involve in the process, in the same room at the same time, is the fastest path to alignment. Despite any agreement you've made, however, the Consensus Builder may still get cold feet, so as soon as you get alignment, lock it down in writing.

Energizer

Energizers are the opposite of Analyzers. Where Analyzers are linear and methodical, Energizers are nonlinear, disorganized, and scattered. The best way to describe the Energizer is fire, ready, aim.

They easily get off track and can burn a significant amount of time at the negotiation table on nonrelated issues. To keep things on track, it is important that you start with a clear agenda and follow up with written communication confirming any verbal agreements.

Energizers make great coaches and champions because they enjoy connecting with people and sharing information. If you get into a bind, they can help you influence other stakeholders to take your side.

They value relationships. Unlike Directors and Analyzers, with Energizers it's the relationship first and then business. They tend to communicate in long stories, are emotional and animated, and have high energy along with a high need to be appreciated.

They like to be the center of attention. They love compliments and flattery and feel most appreciated when they're talking and you are listening. This need to feel appreciated must not be discounted. Energizers will agree to concessions at the negotiation table just because they like you. When you listen to them, they'll work with you. Their insatiable need to feel important often overrides objective, rational decision making.

Salespeople damage relationships with Energizers when they compete for space in the conversation. When you work with an Energizer, it's critical to keep your eye on the prize; focus on the outcome you want rather than your own need for attention.

When you negotiate with Energizers, the key is to control the conversation with open-ended questions that keep them talking and allow you to guide the conversation without making them feel that you are cutting them off.

Director

Directors make decisions quickly. They have a strong bias toward action and are most comfortable working with sales professionals who get things done.

They crave control. If you want them to like you, do not compete with them. Even when Directors have given decision-making authority to another person, they'll swoop in at the last minute and subtly exert control by "putting their stamp on it."

Salespeople sometimes sink deals in these situations because they pick fights with Directors who may challenge them directly—not because the Director doesn't agree with the decision their subordinate has made but because they want to ensure that everyone knows who is boss.

The Director values confidence. They steamroll insecure salespeople with no compunction. If you don't have an answer to a question, do not try to fake it, do not stumble over your words, and do not act weak or scared. If you do, the Director will first lose respect for you and then flatten you. Instead, confidently say you don't know but will get back to them with the answer. Give a specific time when you will give them the answer, and do not miss that commitment.

Directors have no patience for long-winded explanations. When you make your case at the negotiation table, do so with bullet points and short, concise messages. Give them a little bit of information, pause and check, then give a little bit more, and pause and check.

If you waste a Director's time, you lose them. When you say anything that is not relevant to their situation, you lose them. They care about their problems and issues and how you can solve them.

Directors can be demanding and intimidating in sales negotiations. At times, they will challenge, push, and negotiate hard just to see if you can take it. When you stand your ground and demonstrate respectful confidence while careful not to challenge their authority, they will respect you. This opens the door to alignment on an agreement.

It is possible to build deep, trusting relationships with Directors, but it is business first, get stuff done (GSD), and socialize last. However, when they feel that you can be counted on to follow through on your promises, they will buy from you and keep buying from you.

Stranger Danger and the Procurement Pit

One of the most disconcerting situations you will encounter is a stranger who is brought in to negotiate the final deal with you. The stakeholder group selects you as the VOC and then ushers you off to these strangers.

Funding buyers, like a purchasing professional, an attorney, or even a CFO, may be brought into the process late in the game. You are not likely to have a relationship with these individuals and are often treated as an insignificant annoyance.

One reason that big companies bring in procurement to negotiate deals is that the strangers in procurement are emotionally disconnected from the outcome. They don't care about your past relationships or any agreements that you may have made. They have a basic function: to extract as many price concessions from you as possible and force you to accept contractual terms and conditions that favor their organization.

This "stranger danger" is especially hard on sales professionals with an Energizer communication style (which most salespeople have). Energizers count on their ability to build emotional connections and relationships for leverage at the sales negotiation table.

Because these salespeople depend so much on relationships for leverage, they instantly lose all of their ammunition when a stranger is brought in to negotiate the deal. To make things worse, the stranger is often a professional negotiator (typically with a string of acronyms following their name) with an Analyzer persona—kryptonite for the Energizer salesperson.

At the table, the Analyzer shows little emotion and is not swayed by the salesperson's attempts to connect. The Analyzer demonstrates relaxed, assertive confidence and methodical intent, focusing on the facts and figures. In another form of rope-a-dope, they slowly but surely wear the salesperson down and drain their negotiation leverage while giving few real concessions. The salesperson becomes frustrated and emotional. Then they get crushed.

Getting forced into the procurement pit sucks. It's dehumanizing and robs you of your self-respect. This is why early in the sales process, I ask this qualifying question:

"Once you and I have an agreement, what happens next?"

If the final negotiation of the deal is going to procurement, I want to know early. This allows me to make important decisions about my next steps and develop a strategy for dealing with procurement.

When new stakeholders come into the picture at the negotiation phase, you will need to lean on your coaches and executive sponsors for information about these people.

When I'm put in the position of negotiating with a stranger, I leverage a negotiation triangle between me, my executive sponsor, and procurement. This triangle allows me to play hardball with the strangers in procurement and strengthen my power position by leveraging my executive sponsor to back me up and remove procurement's alternatives.

Most importantly, you must know your numbers. Be prepared to make your case with math, build lock-tight value bridges, and allow your business case to do the talking.

29

Empathy and Outcome: The Dual Process Approach

You've learned that effective sales negotiation is the process of winning for your team *and* preserving the relationship. But the objective is *not* the relationship. The goal of effective sales negotiation is making a profitable deal for your company and delivering value to your customer.

Don't get me wrong—relationships matter. I just want to be crystal clear that your goal is inking a good deal. Salespeople who forget this truth are doomed to mediocrity because they're good at making friends and bad at negotiating outcomes that maximize profit for their company, value for their customers, and income for themselves.

Salespeople who fall into this trap are often exceptional at perceiving and responding to the emotions of others. People like them, and they are eager to please people. But they blow it in sales negotiations because the relationships keep getting in the way. They believe that "win–win" equates to the other side of the table being happy.

Because they cannot regulate their disruptive emotional need to be liked and accepted, they hand over the company's profits and their commission check to these "friends" who are more than happy to take it. Their eagerness to please stakeholders derails them at the negotiation table.

At the sales negotiation table, you are there to make deals, not friends. The outcome you seek is not the relationship. It's negotiating the best deal possible for your team.

This does not mean that the relationship isn't important. You cannot operate in a vacuum, focusing solely on the self-centered outcome you want.

You cannot ignore the human and emotional component inherent in sales negotiation. The stronger your relationship with the stakeholders and the more people like you as a person, the higher the probability that you will align on an agreement, ink the deal, retain the account, and maximize the lifetime value of your customer.

You must not lie, manipulate, act without integrity, take unfair advantage of the other party, or negotiate in ways that create resentment for either party. You must not become so attached to winning that you miss opportunities to compromise, turn people off, lose deals, and destroy relationships.

Sales EQ and Dual Process Communication

Master sales negotiators have developed a high Sales EQ—*sales-specific emotional intelligence.* Sales EQ is the balance of being aware of and rising above your own disruptive emotions while also accurately sensing, understanding, and appropriately responding to the emotions of others.

Effective negotiators leverage Sales EQ to equalize the investment in interpersonal relationships *and* achieving their primary objective of winning for their team. It's a dual process of *empathy* for their stakeholder's position and a drive for *outcome*.

F. Scott Fitzgerald said that "the test of a first-rate intelligence is the ability to hold two opposed ideas in mind at the same time and still retain the ability to function." Dual process is the mental and emotional acuity to stand in the stakeholder's shoes, viewing things from their perspective (empathy), while at the same time focusing on your negotiation objective—winning for your team.

It's one of the most difficult emotional challenges for sales professionals.

- It's not pleasing your buyers at all costs—believing that you are either for your stakeholders or against them.
- Nor is it the cold, calculated approach of narcissistic manipulators—focusing on extracting as much from the stakeholders as possible, in the shortest amount of time, with the least amount of emotional investment.

We all possess empathy—the capability of relating to the emotions of others.

- Along with emotional self-control, empathy is a meta-skill in sales negotiations.
- Empathy is the ability to step into your stakeholder's shoes and experience emotions from their perspective. It allows you to identify with their feelings and motivations.
- Empathy gives you insight into the perspectives of the people you are negotiating with.

From this perspective, effective negotiators can step back from the emotional cauldron of the sales negotiation table and find unique paths to negotiated outcomes while still protecting their profits and paychecks.

When used correctly, empathy helps you avoid intentionally injuring other people. It lets you look into the future and helps you become aware that a potential action or concession may create resentment and contempt down the road.

Yet, empathy may also become a disruptive emotion that costs you dearly in negotiations if it causes you to give away the farm out of eagerness to please other people or (even worse) project the size of your wallet onto the buyer.

The Problem with Projecting

A few years back, my wife and I bought our dream home. It was on a stretch of farmland—exactly what we'd always wanted. We both knew in our hearts that it would be the last home we ever bought. This was where we planned to spend the rest of our lives.

This house, however, had to be completely remodeled. The work was so extensive that the contractor estimated that it would take eighteen months before we could even move in.

Through the years, Carrie and I had remodeled eleven houses. Each time, we'd done the work on a tight budget and made sacrifices to stay within budget. This time, though, we had the budget to create the home that we wanted. We promised ourselves there would be no shortcuts and no compromises. We planned to do it right.

After months of work, we were finally finishing up the bathrooms, and it was time to order the glass doors for the showers. The representative for the glass company met us at the house. We carefully explained exactly what we wanted. He gathered measurements and took notes.

The last stop was the bathroom in our master bedroom. He collected the measurements and started writing up the order. As he did, a worried look crossed his face, and he shook his head. Then he looked up said, "You know, all this custom work is going to be really expensive. Are you sure you don't want to go with our standard doors? It will save you a ton of money."

"Like how much more?" I asked

"At least 20%. Probably more," he responded, still shaking his head.

He clearly missed that the walls and floors of the newly remodeled bathroom had freshly installed imported marble costing more than $30,000. Rather than upselling and showing us even more options, he was negotiating down, projecting the size of his wallet on us instead of focusing on the size of ours.

Projecting, which is all too common for salespeople, will cost you dearly at the sales negotiation table. When you negotiate with the size of your wallet, you routinely apologize for your prices, give concessions without being asked, and decide for your buyers what they can afford.

Empathy Scale

Each person occupies a unique place on the empathy scale. For some people, empathy comes easily, whereas for others it requires intentional effort.

My wife, for example, is highly empathetic. She doesn't need to work hard to feel what other people are feeling. I, on the other hand, am naturally egocentric. Because of this trait, I must consciously work to remain aware of my emotional blind spots and be intentional with my efforts to be empathetic.

Your natural level of empathy is mostly innate—it's baked into your genes. So it's necessary to be honest with yourself about how you view the world. Although you cannot change your natural level of empathy, you can rise above it and choose how you approach other people.

Are you more other-focused, like my wife, or more self-focused, like me? Most people fall somewhere in the middle of the empathy scale—3 and 4 for the self-centric crowd and 6 and 7 for the other-focused (Figure 29.1).

Figure 29.1 The Empathy Scale.

One way to know where you sit on the empathy scale is to consider how you tend to interpret the behaviors, communication styles, and emotions of other people. Your snap judgments reveal a great deal about how tuned in you are to their emotions. People tend to interpret the behavior of others in two general ways:

- **Situational attributions:** Upon observing a person who is angry, you interpret this to mean that he or she is having a bad day or experiencing a difficult circumstance.
- **Dispositional attributions:** Upon observing a person who is angry, you believe that his or her underlying personality is the cause and subsequently label that person an asshole or a jerk.

People who interpret human behavior based on situational attributions tend to be more empathetic than those who rely on dispositional attributions and labels.

Be Intentional

The first step to mastering the Dual Process is to become aware of where you sit on the empathy scale. In other words, to tune in effectively to the emotions of others, you must first become adept at tuning in to your own emotions and acknowledging your blind spots. The next step is rising above your DNA and choosing your intentions.

- **Intentional Empathy:** If you are more outcome-driven, like me, you must intentionally focus on listening, being patient, paying attention to nuance, and tuning in to the feelings of others.

- **Intentional Outcome Drive:** If you are more empathetic, like my wife, you must be intentional about avoiding projection, being assertive, asking for what you want, and locking down agreements.

People lower on the empathy scale tend to be better at directly asking for what they want and locking down commitments, but they are poor listeners, impatient, and self-focused.

If this describes you, before you go into a sales negotiation conversation, you must consciously decide to become other-focused when interacting with stakeholders. You must intentionally and actively choose to:

1. Listen to stakeholders with all your senses (ears, eyes, and intuition)
2. Give stakeholders your complete attention
3. Work to view things from their perspective
4. Be concerned with how they feel
5. Find consensus solutions to roadblocks

People on the higher end of the empathy scale tend to be better at listening, understanding, and building connections with other people. Yet they find it emotionally difficult to face conflict, confidently explain their position, ask for what they want, and lock down agreements.

If you are such a person, you must prepare in advance for sales negotiations and make a conscious, intentional decision about how you will defend your position and exactly what you will ask for. You must intentionally choose to:

1. Develop a target outcome in advance and confidently take control of conversations by setting the agenda
2. Avoid projecting
3. Know what you want and ask for it
4. Practice articulating and standing up for your position
5. Demonstrate relaxed, assertive confidence—even when you feel the opposite

Sales professionals who are adroit at leveraging the Dual Process of empathy and outcome are masters at managing their disruptive emotions when negotiating. They are empathetic and understanding, connect with stakeholders at the emotional level, and invest in relationships. Yet they detach from their egocentric need to be liked so they can successfully negotiate profitable deals and win for their team.

How Empathetic Are You?

Test your empathy with these free empathy assessments:
- http://greatergood.berkeley.edu/quizzes/take_quiz/14
- https://psychology-tools.com/empathy-quotient/

---

30 | Seven Keys to Effective Listening

At the strategic level, sales negotiation is like a chess game, but at the tactical level, it's like playing poker. The parties hide their emotions behind poker faces, attempt to obscure the strength of their real hand, sometimes bluff, and keep their cards close to the vest.

The most effective way to get a peek at those cards is to keep your ears open and your mouth shut.

Listening builds deep emotional connections with other people. The more you listen, the more connected your stakeholder will feel to you. As this emotional connection deepens, their trust in you grows, and emotional walls crumble. As the walls come down, they talk more. The more they talk, the more they reveal. This gets you below the surface and lets you access their cards. Listening is where effective sales negotiators earn their stripes.

Yet, listening remains the most underappreciated and under-utilized tactic in sales negotiation. Many ill-informed salespeople believe that to control the sales negotiation, they must be doing the talking. Rather than listening, they are formulating what they plan to say to convince the other party to accede to their position.

Listening is the weakest link in interactions with stakeholders at the negotiation table. We don't listen because it is hard work. It requires empathy, cognitive focus, and a conscious effort to manage our self-centered desire to interrupt and talk over the other person.

Effective listening is the ability to actively understand information expressed by the buyer while causing them to feel that you are paying attention, are interested, and care. It is controlling your disruptive emotions, being empathetic, and avoiding interrupting.

It is listening with the intent to understand, rather than a desire to respond. There are seven keys to effective listening at the sales negotiation table.

Be Prepared

You may have noticed that preparation is a theme repeated in this book. There is a reason for this. Preparation puts you in a position to win. Before all sales negotiation conversations, know your objective and agenda, and be ready with the questions you will ask to clarify and isolate the other side's issues. Prepare yourself to flex to your stakeholders' preferred communication styles.

Be Intentional

Commit to listening. Choose to be a good listener. Choose to be other-focused. Focusing completely on the person in front of you and being genuinely interested is an intentional behavior. Be aware of any disruptive emotions that impede your ability to effectively listen. Determine to rise above them.

Be Present

Be there. Be present in the conversation. Do not allow your mind to wander. Center your mind and focus 100% of your attention on the other person. When you fail to focus on the person you are interacting with, you are on the fast track to turning them off and breaking the emotional connection.

Attention Control

In today's demanding work environment, it is easy to become distracted. We are constantly looking at our devices. Phone calls interrupt conversations. Email, text messages, and social media distract us.

If you've ever been in a conversation with another person who looks away, gets distracted by something or someone else, or interrupts your conversation to return a text message or email, you know how disrespected this makes you feel.

When you believe the other person is not listening to you, it hurts your feelings, makes you feel unimportant, and can make you angry. Just imagine how difficult it becomes to gain alignment on a negotiated agreement when the buyer feels this way about you.

Whenever you interact with a stakeholder in a sales negotiation, be there. Be present in the conversation. Turn everything else off, remain completely focused, and do not let anything distract you. Turn the sound off on devices so that beeps, dings, and buzzes don't cause you to look away. The moment you make the mistake of looking away, not only will you lose concentration, but you'll also offend the other person.

This is especially true on video calls, because the stakeholders have no insight into your environment and will usually assume the worst—that you are not interested in them. When meeting face-to-face, maintain eye contact. When you are on the phone, keep your eyes off papers and screens so you avoid the burning temptation to multitask.

Controlling your eyes keeps you there physically, even when you are on the phone, because where your eyes go, your attention follows.

Active Listening

Active listening is a set of behaviors that provide tangible proof that you are listening. These behaviors include eye contact, acknowledging others with verbal feedback and body language, summarizing and restating what you have heard, and using pauses and silence before speaking. Because listening rewards your stakeholder for talking, it keeps them talking. And the more they talk, the more they'll reveal their cards.

Summarizing, restating, and asking relevant follow-up questions that build on the conversation validate that you are paying attention. Nodding your head, smiling in approval, and leaning forward when you find something they say particularly interesting all demonstrate that you are engaged.

Deep Listening

People communicate with far more than words. To truly hear another person, you must listen with all your senses—eyes, ears, and intuition. This is called deep listening.

When you open your senses to become aware of the entire message, you have the opportunity to analyze the emotional nuances of the conversation. As you listen, observe the other person's body language and facial expressions. You don't need to be an expert in body language to see obvious clues. You only need to be observant and tune in to the emotional nuances.

Pay attention to the tone, timbre, and pace of the stakeholder's voice. Focus on the meanings behind the words they use. Be alert for emotional cues—both verbal and nonverbal. Use this information to flex to their preferred communication style.

When the stakeholders show their emotions through facial expressions, body language, tone, or words, you gain insight into what is *important to them—or what they may be hiding.* Whenever you perceive something that seems emotionally important, ask follow-up questions to test your hunch. This may give you a peek at their cards.

It is easier to connect, keep people engaged, and make them feel important when they are talking about themselves. This opens the door for relevant follow-up questions that encourage your stakeholder to openly discuss the issues that are most important to them—a key to triggering the self-disclosure loop.

Pause Before You Speak

Be careful not to cut the other person off by blurting out your ideas or interrupting them. Pause and count to three before you speak. Leave room for the other person to continue talking, thus activating the self-disclosure loop.

31 | Activating the Self-Disclosure Loop

You tell stories, I tell stories, and your stakeholders tell stories. It's human. It's how we communicate. In conversations, people don't spit out facts in bullet-point lists. Instead, they use stories.

We tell stories to be understood. And, when we are telling our story, we feel important. When you listen attentively, you encourage stakeholders to expand on their stories and tell even more.

But consider your emotional state when another person is telling you their story. Your mind drifts. You feel the urge to jump in and add your two cents. You don't feel important. You experience disruptive emotions.

Stakeholders tell stories to be understood. Within these stories, you gain insight into the buyer's emotions, negotiation strategy, and perceived alternatives.

But you prefer that they communicate in bullet points, because it's easier for you. You want to speed them up and get them to the point, so you can get back to negotiating.

Resist this disruptive emotion. Your stakeholder wants to talk. Don't get in the way. Remember that inside their story are clues that lead to the cards they are holding and a path to an agreement.

Harvard researchers Diana Tamir and Jason Mitchell discovered that humans get a neurochemical buzz from telling stories and self-disclosure.[1] In this fascinating study,[2] subjects were given the opportunity to talk or brag about themselves while their brain activity was being observed on high-powered 3-D magnetic resonance imaging (MRI) scans.

When the subjects began talking about themselves, even about mundane information, the area of the brain associated with pleasurable feelings and rewards became activated. Each time the subject made a self-disclosure, this area of the brain would light up like a Christmas tree.

The subjects were, in fact, getting a shot of dopamine for talking about themselves. And thus a loop was formed. Each revelation of personal information, each brag, each opinion was rewarded with another shot of dopamine, thus encouraging more self-disclosure. This is how conversations can quickly escalate from small talk into too much information (TMI).

You've witnessed this dopamine-triggered self-disclosure loop at parties, family reunions, or even conversations with a stranger at a bar. The other person tells you a little bit about themselves, and you listen. Then they tell a little bit more and a little bit more, until they suddenly cross into the TMI zone, and you're left wondering why in the world they told you something so personal or revealing.

To them, the self-revelation felt great. Even though they consciously knew that they should not say the things they told you, they couldn't help it. It was the dopamine talking. For sales professionals, learning how to activate this self-disclosure loop is one of the secrets to effective information gathering and discovery.

Five Steps to Activating the Self-Disclosure Loop

Activating the self-disclosure loop is a powerful tactic in sales negotiation conversations. When you master it, you'll easily gain insight into the cards in your stakeholder's hand. This insight gives you a distinct advantage at the negotiation table. There are five steps to activating the self-disclosure loop:

1. Begin with easy, open-ended questions that get the other person talking.
2. Use active listening techniques to reward them for talking.
3. Avoid interrupting, rushing, or talking over your stakeholder.
4. Pause three to five seconds before speaking. Allow the stakeholder to fill in the silence. This is important, because if you start talking, you'll break the loop and turn your stakeholder off.
5. Once the loop is running and the stakeholder begins to self-disclose, listen deeply and center your follow-up questions on those self-disclosures.

Activating the self-disclosure loop relies on your ability to remain in the moment. Your questions must be conversational and relevant, organically built upon the conversation and centered on emotion.

Open-ended questions that are easy to answer and asked early in the conversation are the key to activating the buyer's self-disclosure loop. You must get out of the way and allow nature to take its course. Instead of asking one interrogating question after another, as salespeople often do in a drive to get to a quick outcome, leverage the dual process approach to keep the conversation organic and allow it to build on itself.

Don't Interrupt

One sure way to break the self-disclosure loop is to blurt out your next question or statement or, even worse, talk over a stakeholder before they have finished speaking. Nothing makes your stakeholder feel like you aren't listening more than talking over them.

It becomes transparent that you are not listening to understand but are only formulating the next thing you plan to say. When you feel that the other person has finished speaking, pause and count to three.

Pausing leaves room for others to finish speaking and prevents you from cutting them off if they have not. You'll often find that this moment of silence triggers stakeholders to continue talking and reveal important information they were holding back. Like a magnet, silence pulls people toward you and brings what they are hiding to the surface.

The Origin of Influence

Influence at the sales negotiating table is derived from what you hear, rather than what you say. This is why no skill or tactic at the table is more important than listening.

Listening:

- Gets you below the emotional surface
- Reveals what the buyer's poker face is hiding
- Creates the path to agreement by opening the door to common ground
- Allows you to step into the buyers' shoes with empathy and craft value bridges that make sense to them
- Teaches you what to give and what to take

When you learn to communicate effectively in sales negotiations, you'll make fewer mistakes, waste less time because of misunderstandings, gain more influence, pull buyers toward you, turn them into advocates, easily align on agreements, and close many more deals at higher prices with better terms and conditions.

The DEAL Sales Conversation Framework

32 | A Seat at the Table

Let's take a moment a review what we've learned so far about sales negotiations.

- Sales negotiations are different from other forms of negotiation.
- It is in your best interest to master sales-specific negotiation skills.
- You must win first and then negotiate.
- If you make concessions when you have not been implicitly or explicitly selected as the vendor of choice (VOC), you are negotiating with yourself.
- Sales negotiation is about winning for your team while minimizing resentment at the same time; in sales, relationships matter.
- Motivation, leverage, and power position form the chess board of sales negotiation.

- Buyers almost always begin with a stronger power position than sellers.
- Leverage lets you shape buyer behaviors, and you must never give it away for free.
- Power at the negotiation table is derived from alternatives.
- Sales process excellence and effective discovery improve your power position.
- You must master your emotions in order to master sales negotiation.
- The more you need the deal, the more you will give away to get it.
- A full pipeline lowers your desire to make concessions and gives you greater emotional self-control.
- In every sales negotiation conversation, the person who exerts the greatest emotional control has the highest probability of achieving their desired outcome.
- Emotions are contagious, and people respond in kind.
- The most powerful negotiating position is relaxed, assertive confidence.
- Sales negotiation planning prepares you mentally and emotionally to gain an advantage at the negotiation table.
- Influence at the sales negotiation table is derived from what you hear rather than what you say.

Now we're going to take a seat at the table and engage in a sales negotiation conversation.

The DEAL Sales Negotiation Conversation Framework

In a world where buyers almost always have more alternatives, a stronger power position, and are better trained to negotiate than you, without a plan and framework to guide you, it's easy to:

- Lose control of the conversation and become the buyer's puppet
- Become impatient or fearful, so that you give in too soon or make more concessions than required to close the deal

- Become insecure, flustered, and embarrassed when you get bullied or pushed around
- Allow your emotions to control you rather than rising above them and intentionally choosing your response
- Negotiate the wrong issues
- Give high-value concessions without getting equal or greater value back from the buyer
- Succumb to the games that buyers play

In the previous sections, we discussed strategy, planning, preparation, and communication principles. In sales negotiations, you need a plan, because winging it is stupid. But, of course, sales negotiation plans, like most battle plans, rarely survive first contact.

This is why you must also deploy a tactical framework that guides the actual negotiation conversation so you remain agile, flexible, in control, and on track to achieve your goal.

There are four parts of the DEAL Sales Negotiation Conversation Framework (Figure 32.1):

1. **Discover.** Get the buyer's issues, desires, concerns, and perceived alternatives on the table. Then, clarify and isolate the issues on their list that must be negotiated, while seeking common ground.
2. **Explain.** Make the case for the value of your proposal by building a value bridge from it to the stakeholder group's desired business outcomes and the metrics that matter.
3. **Align.** Run your give-take playlist to give appropriate concessions and make take-aways until you reach alignment on a mutual agreement.
4. **Lock.** Ask for an explicit commitment on any agreements reached in the alignment step. Get INK.

Although the DEAL framework can be a linear progression in simple situations with a single issue, in most sales negotiations it's more of a loop than a line.

In complex negotiations, you may run through the framework multiple times across many issues, locking down one agreement at a time. In other cases, you'll go back and forth between

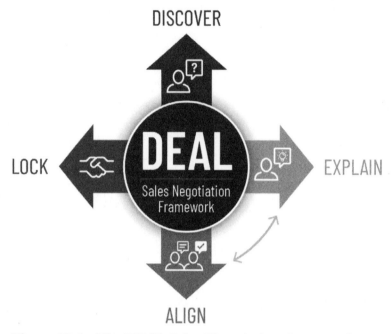

Figure 32.1   The DEAL Sales Negotiation Conversation Framework.

explaining your position, bridging to value, and aligning on negotiated agreements.

Leveraging this framework keeps you on track, no matter what
the buyer hits you with. The DEAL framework enables you to be
agile in the moment and to flex easily to the context of the situation without locking you into a one-size-fits-all box. It guides the
sales negotiation conversation and keeps you moving toward alignment on a negotiated outcome.

33 | Discover

The objective of the discover step of the DEAL Sales Negotiation Conversation Framework is getting the buyer's list of issues on the table and isolating and clarifying those issues before explaining your position. The key to this step is keeping your eyes and ears open and your *mouth shut.*

The DEAL framework as explained on paper is a simple, straight forward four-step process:

1. The buyer explains their position.
2. You explain your position.
3. Then you give and take until you come to an agreement.
4. Finally, you lock it down with a handshake and ink.

It would be awesome if it worked this smoothly in the real world. But it doesn't. Buyers don't always follow the rules. They don't always carefully and clearly articulate their position. They don't start with a focus on collaboration, consensus, and alignment. Instead they hit you right up front and in the face with demands for concessions. They:

- Demand that you lower your prices
- Demand that you change your terms and conditions
- Ask for free stuff
- Say things like, "There's no way I'm paying that much!" or "We're not signing a five-year contract!" or "Your competitors are much lower than you!"
- Throw all their alternatives in your face
- Diminish the value of your recommendations and business outcome map
- Pick on any flaw they can find in your business case, product, or service
- Tell you that you're just the same as your competitors
- Complain to you that they don't have enough budget
- Point out a bad online review of your company

Savvy buyers will put anything on the table and use any tactic they feel will improve their power position and give them the leverage to win for their team.

The discover step gives you the space necessary to control your emotions and patiently ask questions to clarify the other side's position so you can find common ground and isolate what must be negotiated.

Buyers have been taught negotiation skills and basic human psychology. They've learned the common patterns of salespeople at the negotiation table and how to trigger their emotions, gain control of the conversation, and play them like a fiddle.

When you understand the games buyers play and are aware of when these tactics are being aimed at you, that knowledge helps you avoid becoming a victim and allows you to remain in control of the conversation.

Bullying

Some buyers will attempt to bully you and push you into making quick concessions. They'll come at you hard with sharp demands and take extreme positions. They may attack your integrity, take an aggressive physical stance, attempt to intimidate you, or try to overpower you with rapid-fire communication and a harsh tone of voice.

This tactic is most often used by the Director buyer persona. It works with desperate salespeople who fold easily under pressure, and with sales professionals who are higher on the empathy scale to whom it feels like an attack.

This buyer behavior can shake your confidence and trigger insecurity. If you are are more outcome-driven than other-focused, it can trigger arguments and attempts to defend your position. In either event, if you engage with a bully, you cede your emotional discipline to the buyer and lose control of the conversation.

The most effective way to neutralize a bully is to ignore the tactic. Give it no oxygen. Show no emotion. Respond with a non-complementary behavior—relaxed, assertive confidence. Once bullies see that the tactic isn't working, they'll change their behavior and respond in kind.

Triggering Obligation

Some buyers will sweet-talk you. Buyers with an Energizer communication style are masters at this tactic. They'll tell you how much they like you. Give you compliments. Congratulate you on doing a great job with the presentation. Laugh and joke. And once they've connected with you emotionally, they reel you in and ask you to "help them out" (as you would a friend) with a concession.

The most insatiable human need is the feeling of significance or importance. Robert B. Cialdini, author of *Influence*, says, "One of the most potent of the weapons of influence around us is the rule for reciprocation. The rule says that we should try to repay, in kind, what another person has provided us."[1]

In layman's terms, the law of reciprocity simply explains that when someone gives you something—like a sincere compliment at the beginning of a sales negotiation—you feel an obligation to give value back. When the buyer makes you feel important, it triggers a subconscious feeling of obligation. This feeling increases the probability that you will give an early concession and ask for nothing in return.

This feeling of obligation, the need to reciprocate, is baked deep into human psychology. It is so hardwired into our emotions that it makes us easy to get played. The most effective defense is preparation and a well-thought-out sales negotiation map (SNM). Your SNM puts hard brackets around possible concessions and, when combined with a Give-Take Playlist, helps you avoid making unnecessary concessions.

The good news is that reciprocity goes both ways. When you are kind, respectful, empathetic, and sincerely focused on listening to your stakeholder, it makes them feel important. When you give them this gift, they also feel the need to reciprocate, which increases the probability that you will find consensus and align on an agreement.

Sympathy

Some buyers are especially good at pulling your sympathy strings. It's poor mouth and poor me—often combined with a compliment to create obligation.

They'll tell you all their problems and why they can't do the deal on your terms. They'll say you need to cut them a break, help them out while they get things going, or work with them until they get more budget.

Sometimes a concession may be the right thing to do, but generally you'll end up resenting the other party, because your sympathy is rarely rewarded with more business and loyalty.

Salespeople high on the empathy scale are particularly susceptible to this ploy, as are those who are desperate to sell anything.

When you are working with such buyers, put on your Teflon skin and do not allow their problems to become your problems. Stick to your game plan and make them focus on the value you are delivering. If they still can't afford you, move on—you should never have been in this poorly qualified deal in the first place.

Guilt

Buyers will sometimes attempt to use guilt to get concessions from you. They may point out a mistake you made or some other misstep and use it as leverage to compel you to give them a concession to make up for it.

In a particularly nefarious ploy, some buyers—especially those from procurement—will say things like:

> *We really like you, but your boss (or other team member) ruffled feathers around here. Some people on the team were offended by his tone and the way he communicated. He came close to getting you eliminated from the consideration process. I really like you, though, and want to give you a chance. But I'm going to need you to work with me on this pricing so we can keep you in the game.*

I've watched salespeople (especially those salespeople with a Consensus Builder communication style) panic when they get these calls. All they can think of is finding a way to make it up to the buyer. But it's only a ploy; the buyer is trying to use guilt to gain concessions from emotionally gullible salespeople.

Your best defense against guilt tactics is to ignore them and stick with your sales negotiation plan. It's a challenge because this ploy is so emotional, but it's the only effective way to deal with attempts to use guilt as leverage.

If for some reason ignoring it gets you eliminated from the deal, so be it. Trust me, you do not want to work with such an organization or such people over the long-term.

The at Carrot Gambit and FOMO

One of the most common emotional tugs for salespeople is the carrot gambit. I've been on the losing end of this one, as have most salespeople. It is very difficult to manage your emotions when a seemingly sincere buyer says something like:

> *We really like you, and there are some big projects coming up next year that we'd like to give you. We're hoping you can give us a price break on this contract so we can get to know you better and introduce you to the other people in our company.*

Likewise, there is the buyer who uses FOMO—the fear of missing out. They let you in on insider information about a big budget increase, a new division, new markets, or big changes that give you the opportunity to get in and make a big sale. They insinuate that you'll find it easier to get a shot at this opportunity if you are already on the inside.

It's always the same game. Give us a break on your prices now (give us a pilot, trial, sample), and we'll give you a shot a lot more business later.

It's funny how it never works out that way. And if you do make an initial concession on your price—just to get your proverbial foot in the door—it is very difficult to raise your prices on future contracts.

The "carrot gambit" is where dreams of big deals go to die. The most effective way to deal with this tactic is awareness that the carrot being dangled in front of you is most likely a red herring—with the fishy smell to go along with it. Treat it that way, and don't chase it.

If you do feel that the future opportunities are real, use your leverage (concessions) to get written commitments for those opportunities.

Disruptive Emotions Can Hit You Like a Ton of Bricks

Regardless of how buyers approach you early in the sales negotiation, the disruptive emotions that follow can hit you like a ton of bricks. You may feel as if you've been punched in the gut. Your brain turns off. You stumble over your words. You feel out of control. In this state, there are four possible responses:

- Counter
- Capitulate
- Confront
- Clarify

Counter

Especially when you get anchored (when the buyer changes the anchor point of the negotiation from your proposal to a new, much lower number), your first reaction is often to make a quick counteroffer *before*:

1. Clarifying why the buyer made such a low-ball offer
2. Diffusing the anchor
3. Explaining your position
4. Considering the unintended consequences of your concession
5. Getting an equal or greater concession in return

You react without thinking. In most situations, you then make a massive and unnecessary early concession, which costs you big time. The reactive counter is most likely to happen when you fail to develop a sales negotiation plan and run through potential scenarios in advance.

Capitulate

In the moment, it may feel easier to just give up and give in. You may be tempted to capitulate to:

- Avoid conflict
- Please the stakeholder and win their approval
- Get a quick, easy win

Sadly, many, many salespeople, especially those seeking the path of least resistance to a commission check, roll over quickly when the negotiation conversation starts. They give away their leverage and minimize their paycheck. They take whatever the buyer will *let* them have.

Just three weeks ago, I was observing one of my client's reps in action on the phone. I listened as he gave away 100% of his negotiation leverage in the first thirty seconds of the conversation.

Buyer (on the phone): "I'd really like to move forward with you on this, but your price is too high. I don't know how you can possibly justify this when your competitors are offering the exact same thing but are $20,000 lower than you."

Me (in my head): *1) If that's true, why are you still talking to us? 2) This is total BS, because the competitors don't have anything comparable to this platform.*

Sales Rep (folding like a cheap lawn chair): "Well I definitely want your business. The most I'm allowed to take off is $8,000. How does that sound?"

Me (in my head but almost out loud): *Noooooooooooooooooooooo!*

Buyer: "That's better, but I know you can do more."

Sales Rep: "Well, I can't, but maybe my manager can. Hold just a second while a make a call."

Me: *Banging my head against the wall.*

Sales Rep: "Good news. I was able to get my manager to come down another $5K. That takes $13,000 off. How does that sound?"

Buyer: "OK! You've got a deal. How do we get this set up?"

This wouldn't be so sad if it wasn't true. But it happens daily in sales negotiation conversations. Salespeople capitulate to buyers' concessions quests without even attempting to negotiate.

Confront

The buyer's approach may feel like an attack. You'll want to argue back and defend your position. Their attempt to draw concessions out of you pisses you off. Perhaps you've been thoughtful and worked very hard to put together a business case that truly solves their problems, and you feel insulted.

Out of frustration, you may want to tell them to go pound sand or that you don't even want their business. You may be tempted to throw your alternatives in their face. "You don't want to do this? Then fine, I have a line of buyers waiting to talk to me!"

In this moment, it's easy to view your stakeholder as an adversary or attempt to prevail in an argument. Especially for salespeople on the lower end of the empathy scale, the first move is often to push back hard, "No. That's not going to happen." You fight and get into a debate.

When we watch negotiation scenes in movies and on TV, the hero is almost always arguing their way to agreement. They draw hard lines in the sand and fight until the other side capitulates. We love it, because it feels good to watch the hero take control and win.

However, this is a poor tactic at the negotiation table. Arguing is one of the ways to damage relationships and create resentment and contempt. When stakeholders are viewed as adversaries you must conquer, negotiation becomes a competition rather than a collaboration.

Arguing doesn't work. It is a basic fact of human behavior that you cannot argue other people into believing that they are wrong. The more you push, the more they'll dig their heels in, become wedded to their position, and resist you.

This behavior is called *psychological reactance.* It is the predictable human tendency to rebel in the face of a debate or when choices are taken away from them. When someone tells you that you're wrong, your response is quick and emotional (even when you really *are* wrong): "Oh, yeah? I'll show you!"

Psychological reactance unleashes your inner brat. No matter the logic of your argument, data, or supporting facts, the people you are arguing with won't suddenly change their mind and agree with you. They become stubborn, illogical, and obstinate.

When you trigger reactance, you push your stakeholder away from you rather than pulling them toward you. When you attempt to explain your position, they can no longer hear you.

Overcoming, combatting, rebutting, and debating do not work. Instead of gaining alignment and agreement, you create animosity, exasperation, and frustration for both you and the other side of the table. This is why you should avoid saying "no" and focus instead on clarifying the situation and then deploying your GTP to find a way forward.

Clarify

There is a better way. When the buyer hits you hard for concessions, you must pause and flip the script. Gain control of the conversation by asking open-ended questions that get them talking about their list of issues.

Slow things down, rise above your emotions, and instead of reacting and responding, patiently get everything on the table before addressing any demands for concessions.

Rise Above Your Emotions and Clarify   When stakeholders ask for concessions or express concerns, it's not always clear what they mean or are asking for. Sometimes they express a concern one way—"your price is too high"—but mean something else—"the subscription for the software is reasonable, but I don't see value in the professional services fee for setting it up."

They may say, "We're not signing a five-year contract." But they mean, "We find your clause for terminating the contract overly burdensome and unclear."

If you begin negotiating or making concessions before you understand what the other party really means or wants, you may end up making the wrong concession (and not being able to get it back), giving away more than required to align on an agreement, or even losing the deal to a perceived better alternative.

Never, ever assume you know what your stakeholder means. Always clarify. When you assume, you lose context. You make mountains out of molehills. Or you miss the real issue all together.

No matter how the buyer approaches the negotiation, you should patiently ask questions that get them talking. Ask open-ended questions like:

> "Can you help me understand what you are trying to accomplish?"
>
> or
>
> "Tell me more."
>
> or
>
> "What problem are you trying to solve?"
>
> or
>
> "Why is this important to you?"

or

"What does success mean to you?"

One of my favorite ways to pull information from buyers is the *statement and pause* approach. I'll say something like, "Wow, it sounds like that's really important to you…" Then I pause and use silence as leverage to do the rest of the work.

Conversely, closed-ended questions elicit short, limited responses and only give you the illusion of control. They require little intellectual or emotional effort from the stakeholder, which makes it easy for them to hide crucial information from you.

Here are some more examples of clarifying questions:

- "I'm just curious. When you say our prices are too high, what does that mean from your standpoint?"
- "Can you help me understand why striking that clause in our contract is so important to you?"
- "What has you concerned about the cost of the training for your users?"
- "When you say that our professional services for setting your program cost too much, how do you mean?"
- "Can you walk me through what's worrying you about this?"
- "How so?" and "How do you mean?" are two of my favorite and most used clarifying questions, because they get people talking.

Isolate the Concern Before Explaining Your Position   Once you get clarification, isolate the concern. Stop and verify you have everything on the table before moving on to explaining your position. Your goal is to get the entire negotiation list out in the open so you know exactly what you are dealing with.

Just pause and ask an isolating question: "With a decision this important, it certainly makes sense that you get the best price. Other than the pricing, though, what else do we need to work out in order to align on an agreement?"

Isolating questions like this one prioritize the importance of the issues on the buyer's negotiation list and put brackets around them. This makes it much easier to narrow the focus of the sales negotiation.

I've said this before, and I'm saying it again for good measure. The secret to getting alignment on an agreement is not what you say—it's what you hear. Listening leads to the INK you seek. It helps you see below the surface and truly understand the issue—especially when you successfully trigger the self-disclosure loop.

There is absolutely nothing more critical to aligning on an agreement than asking great clarifying questions and listening. It is here that the buyer teaches you exactly how to bridge to value and leverage your Give-Take Playlist to both satisfy them and compel them to ink the deal.

W-A-I-T

This past winter, I was negotiating the terms and conditions of a long-term training agreement with a prospective customer's in-house attorney. He had rewritten our intellectual property clause—essentially creating a "work for hire agreement."

The way he worded the language meant that all the work we did for them, including all of our training materials, would become their intellectual property the moment we delivered our training material to his employees. It was a ludicrous clause and an absolute nonnegotiable.

He'd been a bit of a bully about it and it pissed me off. I, in turn, allowed my disruptive emotions to get the best of me and responded in kind with a hard "when hell freezes over" approach.

That "no" triggered reactance, and our negotiation conversation devolved into an argument. We'd each staked out positions, dug in our heels, and were not moving.

Suddenly he raised his voice and started shouting at me, "We want to do business with you, and I don't understand why you are treating me this way!"

His emotional outburst got my attention. In a moment of awareness, I realized that I had explained my position before listening to and clarifying his. He felt that my response had been a personal attack.

In that moment I used an internal question that helps me rise above my emotions, turn my mouth off, and turn my ears on in emotionally tense situations: *W-A-I-T – Why Am I Talking?*

This triggered a simple this–or–that mental process that helped me choose my next move: *"Do I want to win the argument and prove this guy wrong? Or, do I want to ink this deal and make money?"*

I paused, stopped arguing, relaxed my tone, and responded. "I apologize. I can tell that this is very important to you, and I wonder if you might take a moment to help me understand what is worrying you the most and what problem you are trying to solve?"

His tone shifted too, as he responded in kind. "This is a very competitive industry, and we're worried that you'll come in, train our sales team, and then take what you learn from us and teach our competitors."

Instantly, I understood. He was afraid and wanted peace of mind. What he really wanted was an exclusive arrangement. He just didn't know how to ask for it, so his answer had been to lock up our intellectual property.

I responded, "The agreement already contains a mutual nondisclosure clause that protects you and keeps us from sharing your information with anyone. What it sounds like you are looking for, though, is an exclusive relationship so we don't work with any of your competitors."

"Yes, that's it. That's exactly what we want," he responded, in a conciliatory tone.

From there it was easy. First, the exclusive arrangement didn't cost us anything because we had no intention of developing any additional business in his company's industry. It wasn't a sandbox in which we wanted to play. Secondly, it has always been our unwritten policy to avoid conflicts of interest inside highly competitive industries whenever it is possible.

The concession for an exclusive arrangement, therefore, was "funny money"—something that is extremely valuable to the buyer but costs the seller little or nothing.

In exchange for the exclusive agreement (funny money), we inked a three-year rather than a one-year sales training agreement and increased our rate by 25%. It tripled the value of the agreement, which was a big win for our team, and gave him the protection and peace of mind he was looking for.

Use the Ledge

When you get hit hard at the beginning of a sales negotiation, the key is responding with a noncomplementary behavior. Instead of responding in kind to their emotions (moving toward them), respond with relaxed, assertive confidence—your most powerful stance at the sales negotiation table.

When you respond with noncomplementary behavior, it disrupts the other person's pattern, pulls them toward you, and puts you in control. Because it is difficult to control your response in emotionally charged situations, the powerful ledge technique can come to your rescue.

Here are some examples:

Buyer: "Your competitor's price is 20% lower than yours."

You: "I get how it can seem that way and why you are concerned. No one wants to pay more than they should."

Buyer: "We like your proposal, but there is no way we are signing a five-year contract."

You: "I get where you are coming from. Help me understand what's worrying you about that."

Buyer: "We want to do business with you, but your proposal is way out of line."

You: "I think we may be looking at this in very different ways. Why don't we pause for a moment and see where we might find common ground?"

Buyer: "The company that we are working with now doesn't have a service charge. What can we do to take this off your agreement?"

You: "It sounds like this is important to you, especially since you haven't been paying a service charge in the past."

Buyer: "I think we are ready to move forward, but I'm going to need you to help me out and throw in the onboarding and training for our users at no cost."

You: "I'm really glad to hear that you see value in the onboarding training for your users. It's important for helping you to get a quick return on your investment."

Use the ledge to acknowledge that you heard them and relate to them as a person. You are not agreeing to a concession or rolling over. Nor are you discounting their concern, challenging their point of view, judging them, or starting an argument. You are simply relating and affirming, "I get you, and it's OK that you feel this way."

Simple ledge statements like these give your rational brain time to catch up and gain control of your disruptive emotions and also give you time to think and formulate your next move—the magic quarter second.

The ledge slows things down for both parties. Nonjudgmental agreement causes your stakeholders to feel that you are actively interested in understanding them. It grabs their attention and disarms them. This puts you on their side and shifts the conversation from adversarial conflict to collaboration.

34 | Explain Your Position

Step one in the DEAL Sales Negotiation Conversation Framework is asking questions to discover, clarify, and isolate the negotiation list of the stakeholder group or individual buyer. The goal is to get everything on the table that stands in the way of aligning on an agreement and to understand what's most important to the stakeholders.

Once you know what you are dealing with, the next step is to minimize the buyer's concerns by explaining your position in context of the value you are delivering. In particular, one goal is to disrupt the often myopic focus on price. Much of the negotiation is going to center on price. And though price is a ticket to the game, price is not *the game*.

The real game is the value trade. That is, you and your company deliver something of value for the price your prospect pays.

If you executed the sales process effectively, then your presentation and proposal should articulate that value in the context of the stakeholder group's desired business outcomes. The concept of value, though, is often pushed aside by the buyer's fixation on price once you get to the negotiation table.

You may, in fact, have walked the stakeholders through your business case during your presentation twenty minutes earlier. You might have listened as they readily accepted your recommendations, solutions, and planned business outcomes. You celebrated as they said they wanted to do business with you, then watched in awe as amnesia kicked in once the negotiation began.

They forgot that they agreed with your recommendations, the business outcomes they believed you could deliver. They forgot that they were talking to you in the first place because their current vendor was not delivering on promises. And they went straight to "Your prices are 15% more than what we are paying now."

This is when you must know your numbers, know your business case, know the metrics that matter, and know how to articulate these things to protect your position.

Value Versus Price

Value is a simple equation based on measurable business outcomes (MBOs) and emotional business outcomes (EBOs). MBOs may be explained with math, and EBOs are explained by connecting stakeholders to intangibles like peace of mind or their ability to gain time to do the work they truly enjoy.

The value trade is the price your prospect must pay to realize the MBOs and EBOs outlined in your proposal. This is the same value proposition that got you selected—either explicitly or implicitly—as the vendor of choice in the first place. But because buyers have a funny way of forgetting at the sales negotiation table, it will be incumbent on you to be prepared to explain the value again.

Value bridging is the process of helping the buyer understand the value trade—the price they pay (money, terms, and conditions) for the value they receive. This is the return on investment (ROI). It's a simple equation.

ROI = (MBOs + EBOs) − Price

Value bridging is math meeting emotion. The most effective way to bridge from price to the value of MBOs is to use the metrics that matter (MTMs) to your buyer. When a stakeholder challenges the cost (price, terms, conditions) of the value you have proposed, you must be prepared to open your calculator and show them how the numbers work in black and white.

The most effective way to bridge from price to the value of EBOs is to remind them of individual success criteria, challenges, pain, and opportunity by telling their story back to them. In business-to-business sales, stakeholders are almost always using someone else's money to solve their problem.

Go back to the emotional hot buttons and personal success criteria that were disclosed in the discovery phase of the sales process. Use words and phrases that provoke and activate your stakeholder's emotions—typically by relating to painful emotions like stress, worry, insecurity, distrust, anxiety, fear, frustration, or anger, and offering them peace of mind, security, options, hope, a vision for a better future, lower stress, or less worry.

When you can confidently demonstrate your value in relation to price and how the derived value connects to the terms and conditions of the deal, you have the key to maintaining contractual and price integrity and avoiding discounting. For this reason, it is crucial that you prepare by reviewing the deal's Business Outcome Map (Figure 34.1).

BUSINESS OUTCOME MAP & METRICS THAT MATTER			
CHALLENGE	RECOMMENDATION	ASSOCIATED BUSINESS OUTCOMES	METRICS-THAT-MATTER (MTM)
1			
2			
3			
4			
5			

Figure 34.1   The Business Outcome Map.

Price Versus Total Cost of Ownership

The plant manager shook his head at Anthony, "There's no way I can pay this much. At your rates, I'm paying $2.75 more per hour than with your competitor. It's just too much! I'm better off staying where I am."

Anthony took his time. He knew that Keith, the head of operations for a family-owned manufacturer, found it difficult to wrap his head around his proposed *guarantee*. He opened the calculator app on his phone and started doing the math.

"Keith, you told me that this year your line has been down on average four full shifts each month because your current staffing company is unable to get you the operators you need to run your machines. Is that still correct?"

He nodded his head.

"As you explained it, you lose $5,400 an hour when a shift is down." Anthony was entering numbers. "Times eight hours that's $43,200 per shift, and times four that's $172,800 a month. Even with the low hourly rates they give you, you're spending an extra *$173,000* per month." He paused to let that number sink in.

"When we run the numbers on our proposal that increases the hourly rate to $2.75, it's $43,494 more per month than you pay now based on the hourly rate alone. That's a far cry from what it is actually costing you to do business with those other guys. What is most important about our proposal though is our contractual guarantee that you will *always* have enough operators and we will *never* shut down your lines."

Keith thought for a moment, going over the math again in his head. Finally it clicked, and he reached across the table and shook Anthony's hand.

As this story illustrates, in complex deals price is rarely one-dimensional, because there is price and there is total cost of ownership (TCO). In other words, there is the unit price the buyer pays plus the related costs of doing business that must be absorbed over time.

Buyers typically focus on price rather than TCO. With those blinders on, it is difficult for them to see value. For this reason, you need to know your numbers and be prepared to demonstrate the TCO and resulting ROI of your proposal.

Building the Value Bridge

Master negotiators make their case with confident, succinct, personalized bridges built around the buyer's unique situation. The most effective value bridges follow three steps.

1. **Remind them of the problem.** Start with the problems (challenge, need, pain, opportunity) you identified during discovery and articulated in your proposal. Remind them of the problems by telling their story back to them. This is most effective when you also offer data-driven proof of the challenges they face.

2. **Remind them of what they've already agreed to— their yeses.** During your conversations in the sales process, demos, pilots, and your final presentation, the stakeholders agreed on things—the features of your product or service they liked, your recommendations for solving their problems, and the business outcomes they desired. Walk them back through these points of agreement.

3. **Bridge to the value.** Get your calculator out. Show them the math. Connect them to the ROI of anticipated measurable business outcomes. Remind them of what is important to them and use stories about their future state to help them visualize and internalize emotional business outcomes.

When you are explaining your position and bridging to value, remain aware that when your mouth is moving, the buyer's brain is asking two important questions:

"So what?" and *"What's in it for me?"*

If your Value Bridge fails to answer these two questions, it will be difficult to reach alignment on an agreement.

Here's an example of a value bridge. In this situation, Julian is negotiating with Alba, the CFO of a manufacturing organization based in Cleveland, Ohio. Alba is pushing back on the monthly cost of the cloud-based account payables solution that Julian has proposed. She's asked Julian for a discount. This is how Julian demonstrates the value of his solution.

Use the Ledge: *I hear you about how tight margins are in manufacturing, and I know you are worried about adding the expense of the monthly subscription. Two-thousand dollars can seem like a lot, especially when you are paying nothing now.*

Remind them of their problems: *When we met with your accounts payable team, they expressed frustration over the manual process required to sort and pay the invoices that come in each day from multiple vendors. Your controller Ruben said that it was taking up to forty hours of labor each month just to keep it organized. Even with that, he said some invoices are still getting lost, which is requiring them to spend another ten hours doing a monthly audit.*

Just last week your payables team missed a deadline on an early payment rebate that cost you $900. When you and I reviewed the numbers, your best estimate was that the manual processes have caused your team to leave at least $100,000 of payment discounts on the table over the last twelve months.

But the things that seemed to have everyone in the organization frustrated and what was causing you the most stress were the unexpected surprises hitting departmental P&Ls.

Remind them of agreements: *Alba, you agreed that for your company to scale, you need to move to a cloud-based payables platform. In the pilot, your team loved our platform. Rena, your payables manager, said it was the easiest tool she's ever used.*

What had you most excited was the integrated mobile dashboard that gives you and all department heads visibility into the payables that are impacting their P&L. That means you and your team will have the peace of mind that there will be no more embarrassing surprises at the end of the month, and according to Ruben, it will eliminate the need to spend ten hours each month on a complete audit.

Bridge to the value: *But I do get your concern about the price, so let's take a quick look at the math. At a minimum, based on the time saved by eliminating the manual invoice sorting and monthly audits, our product will save a little more than $37,000 in direct payroll costs annually.*

By picking up early payment discounts that you are missing now, you will bring in at least $100,000, which effectively turns payables into a profit center. So just based on the metrics you and your team gave me, you would be investing $24,000 to get an ROI of at least $137,000. Doesn't that seem like a fair trade-off for the cost of the software?

Notice how this example communicates a story. It positions the current untenable situation in stark relief, paints a vivid picture of a better future state (EBO), and demonstrates a tangible return on investment (MBO) all while using Alba's language.

Value bridging is the process of connecting the dots between your solutions and the business outcomes your stakeholders can expect to receive. This must be done in their language, not yours. It is not a features–and–benefits dump.

Know the Numbers

The sales reps in my training room were emphatic that their competitors all sold at a lower price than they did. This, they explained, was why they were at a competitive disadvantage, had to discount so heavily, and were losing sales.

"OK," I said. "I get that. I'm just curious, though. How do you know that your prices are higher than your competitors?"

There was silence in the room. I was staring at them, but they were looking down to avoid making eye contact. It was an argument I'd heard from salespeople dozens of times before. I waited for the answer to come to the surface.

Finally, a young man in the back row raised his hand and spoke the truth, "That's what the stakeholders I'm meeting with keep telling me."

Here is a fact: Buyers generally have more knowledge of the marketplace and competition than salespeople. We can add this to what we've already learned about why buyers are almost always at an advantage and in a better power position than you.

Going into sales negotiations blind is suicidal. At the sales negotiation table, buyers will throw everything they can at you to get a better deal for themselves.

- They'll tell you that your competitors are offering lower prices, better features, higher quality, and more favorable terms and conditions.
- They'll throw their power around by listing their alternatives to doing business with you.
- They'll hit you with market data and trends.

If you hear these things over and over again without checking the facts, it brainwashes you. Like the salespeople in my training room, you begin to believe the buyer's self-serving "truth." And once you have bought in, you become their pawn at the negotiating table.

Effective sales negotiators are students of their marketplace, industry, trends, and competitors. They work hard to know the playing field better than their stakeholders.

Message Matters

When you are explaining your positions and countering those of the buyer, what you say and how you say it matter dearly. You must use confident, direct, and precise language; articulate your position with no hesitation; and know your numbers.

You are the vendor of choice. They have picked you. You've won. Now you must close the deal.

When you are explaining value, complexity is your enemy. When something is hard to grasp, your stakeholder's brain stops paying attention and reverts to the much simpler "but your price is still too high."

The human brain is lazy. It seeks the path of least cognitive load. Humans prefer simple over complex. For this reason, explanations that are complex, ambiguous, or difficult to understand can cause buyers to tune out.

To avoid overwhelming your prospect, keep explanations simple, direct and concise—*less is better.* Practice going through the math before you sit down at the table. Make sure you can build value bridges with no ambiguity. Practice the "So what?" smell test. As you plan for negotiations, where you will defend your value, be prepared to explain your position with a crayon rather than a flow chart.

The goal of explaining your position is getting the buyer to accept your explanation and business case and ultimately agree to the deal. As you explain your position, be careful to avoid words, tone, and posture that the other side might interpret as signs of weakness.

If you are insecure or if your explanation is ambiguous or defensive, they won't trust or believe you, and your value bridge will carry little weight. Instead, like a lion separating the weak gazelle from the herd, the buyer will pounce.

Stakeholders are not judging your message based on *your* intentions. They judge you based on *their* intentions. At the sales negotiation table, you are on stage. Stakeholders are scrutinizing *you*. Your every behavior, every word, every action is being observed. They are looking for congruence in your words, nonverbal communication, and actions. They are observing you for any weakness that can be exploited or anything negative that calls into question your trustworthiness.

Humans focus their attention on things that stick out, and for humans, anything negative sticks out like a sore thumb. This is the *negativity bias*.

The human brain is attuned to what's wrong about someone rather than what is right. Negative perceptions have a greater impact on our responses and behavior than positive ones. Negative messages, thoughts, and images grab and hold our attention.

As you interact with stakeholders, small negative perceptions can add up, building the case that you cannot be trusted. When you lack emotional control, you'll often introduce uncertainty and trigger the negativity bias by:

- Answering unasked questions
- Discussing nonnegotiables even though the prospect hasn't mentioned the issue
- Projecting your fears or the size of your wallet onto the buyer
- Being defensive
- Demonstrating uncertainty
- Giving big concessions too easily and too early
- Struggling to clearly and concisely explain the value trade
- Using insecure, passive, and weak language
- Talking past the explanation because you allow silence to intimidate you

Once your stakeholders begin to believe something is wrong or amiss, they seek out evidence that supports their belief. This *confirmation bias* causes them to be drawn to things that confirm their negative view of you and ask for even more concessions to allay their fear of making a mistake.

35

Align on an
Agreement

Alignment is when all your planning and preparation takes a seat at the table. In the alignment stage of the DEAL framework, you will entertain offers and make counter offers.

The objective of the alignment step is to negotiate an agreement with the buyer while *protecting* your most valuable leverage—those things that negatively impact your income and your company's profit.

Where there is alignment, there is agreement. If the buyer agrees with your value bridge and explanation, you'll shake hands and ink the deal at your proposed prices, terms, and conditions. This is the best-case scenario and your goal.

But sometimes, a point of contention lingers after your explanation. You'll need to make some concessions and work with the buyer to come to an agreement. This process—Discover > Explain

> Align—is fluid. In complex situations it may be repeated on each major issue.

The good news is that when you are negotiating as the vendor of choice and have demonstrated a solid Value Bridge, alignment conversations tend to be collaborative and transparent. Concessions at this point are often about giving the buyer something so they can save face.

Focus on Your Sales Negotiation Map

You are going to make concessions. You are going to give and take on price, terms, and conditions. But as the great Yogi Berra is famous for saying, if you don't know where you are going, you might end up someplace else. When you are negotiating with savvy buyers, that someplace else is usually the place where they reach into your pocket and extract your commission check.

As you shift into the alignment step of the sales negotiation conversation, it's important that you:

- Know the stakeholder group's list and their negotiation parameters
- Inventory your negotiation leverage
- Know your funny money—concessions that cost you little to give but are valuable to the other side
- Have practiced your Give-Take Playlist
- Know your negotiation authority, limits, and nonnegotiables
- Know your target zone and limit zone

Alignment begins and ends with your Sales Negotiation Map (SNM; Figure 35.1). You will build a unique SNM for each deal. The SNM defines and brackets the entire negotiation and serves to keep you on track and on target so that you win for your team.

- The proposal is *your* anchor. It's where the give and take starts. This is your best-case outcome.
- The limit zone is the bottom end. It's where you may end up when you are extremely motivated to ink the deal and are in a weak power position.

Figure 35.1　The Sales Negotiation Map.

- The target zone is your fallback should the buyer not accept your initial proposal. You should be able to back up to the target zone and still deliver a win for yourself and your team.
- The concession zones are where you deploy your Give-Take Playlist. The goal is to leverage the right concessions to satisfy the buyer and protect your profits while leveraging take-aways to compel the buyer to stop negotiating and align on an agreement.

Deploying the Give-Take Playlist

Giving and taking is the art of negotiation. It's the poker game. The game strategy is to leverage concessions that are of low value to you but have high value to the buyer to extract concessions from them that are of high value to you. In the process, your goal is to compel them to agree to a deal (Figure 35.2).

NEGOTIATING LEVERAGE	VALUE TO YOU		VALUE TO STAKEHOLDERS	
	HIGH	LOW	HIGH	LOW

Figure 35.2　Negotiation Leverage Value Inventory.

Figure 35.3   A Give-Take Playlist.

There is a price to pay with each concession. Once that price becomes too high for the buyer, alignment happens. This type of value exchange reduces resentment and protects your profit margins.

When you give, you take (Figure 35.3). You must avoid giving anything away at the sales negotiation table unless you get something back in return. And you are looking for a return that has equal or greater value. For example:

1. If the buyer says that she absolutely cannot live without 90-day payment terms and your proposal is net-30, then you would agree to net-90 only in exchange for a 5% increase on your prices.
2. Or you may agree to 90 days while charging 2% interest on anything outstanding over 60 days, but then offer a 2% rebate when invoices are paid net-30.
3. In exchange for a reduction in price, you ask for an additional term on the agreement.
4. You may reduce the price on a low-profit item in exchange for a larger order of a high-profit item.
5. You will agree to a lower price, but to do so you must remove a contractual guarantee that is important to the buyer.

The give-take plays and combinations of plays are innumerable. The best plays involve funny money. These concessions have low to no cost to you but a high value to the buyer.

Funny money is an effective give-take tactic because it allows you to give something away or take something back that the buyer values without impacting your profit margins. These are often features of your product or service that might be included anyway. Funny money may be held in reserve to use as as leverage or pulled back when the buyer begins pounding you for expensive concessions.

Split your give-take playlist into two parts. Part one is your fallback to the target zone, while part two is your fallback to the limit zone. Set your plays up so that they act as roadblocks that slow the process down. Use small incremental concessions rather than big leaps.

Because every situation is different and sales negotiations can go in multiple directions, you need to be prepared for any scenario. This is where practice makes perfect.

1. Run through the sales negotiation in your head. Practice multiple scenarios.
2. Consider the concessions the buyer may ask for and the moves they might make. Walk through your countermoves.
3. Play out the unintended consequences of each countermove.
4. Build your Give-Take Playlist based on what you believe will create a path to alignment *and* allow you to win for your team.

Pattern Painting

Whenever your give-take behaviors fall into a predictable pattern, you teach buyers how to make counteroffers that perpetuate the pattern. Pattern painting is how you flip the script, change the game, and regain control. It's the act of disrupting expectations with precise numbers and uneven concessions.

Precise Numbers

Studies have demonstrated that when a negotiator makes concessions in round numbers, such as five, then ten, then twenty, those concessions are less likely to lead to alignment than precise numbers. There are two reasons.

First is the brain's tendency to ignore patterns and pay attention to anomalies. It's a simple survival mechanism. We pay attention to things that are out of place because those anomalies could be important—a threat or an opportunity.

Because most sales negotiators operate in round numbers, their pattern is easy to predict and thus fails to grab the buyer's attention. Precise numbers, on the other hand, are unexpected, break the pattern, and therefore are considered more important and thus valuable— pulling the buyer in and forcing them to engage and think.

The second reason, as strange as it might seem, is how precise numbers create the *perception* of confidence. It turns out that when you give the buyer a precise number, such as $26.37 versus $25, they perceive that you are more confident in your numbers. It also causes them to feel that the precise number is less negotiable. This makes it more likely that they will accept your counteroffer and you'll be able to align on a deal.

Irregular Increments

Sellers often fall into a predictable pattern of offering concessions in equal increments. For example, they'll reduce their price in 10% increments or $1,000 increments. These patterns serve as signals to the buyer to keep asking for concessions. Once salespeople move into this pattern it becomes a loop and the most likely outcome is that they keep dropping their price, 10% or $1000 at a time, until they hit their bottom limit.

A better way is to move in irregular increments. For instance, I prefer to begin with a small counter. Suppose my proposal is for $100,000 and my target zone is $90K to $95K. The buyer says they can only pay $80,000.

Rather than taking their bait and getting anchored to $80K, I'll flinch, pause, and counter with $99.3K. My objective is to gauge how much the buyer moves.

Unless the buyer refuses to move, which means that we won't be able to align on a deal, their most likely next step is a much bigger shift toward my position—almost always in a round number. He'll likely move his offer up to $85,000.

To reward him for his generous concession (any behavior that gets a positive reward tends to be repeated) I'll counter with a bigger concession—an additional $2,479. Typically, this compels the buyer to move in another big increment—likely another $5K to $90,000. It is then that I know we are both in sync on my original anchor of $100,000.

My next move is going to be much smaller. This is a signal to him that we are reaching an end. This time I'll drop my price by only another $680 and indicate that it's "all I have to give."

At that point, we'll usually come to an agreement. I called his bluff, diffused his anchor, broke his pattern, remained within my target zone, and delivered a win for my team.

Should the buyer continue to squeeze me for more, I'll leave a long silence between us, say again that "I really don't have that much to give," and then counter with a number that is smaller than my last number. "Really, the most I can help you out with at this point is $490." Then I shut up, wait, and allow silence to become my leverage.

Alternatively, I could pull something back like free delivery or setup in return for the discount, suggest that we move to a different product or solution that will better fit his budget, or use funny money—training, setup, add-ons—in lieu of additional discounts. All are options that you'll want to plan for on your give-take playlist.

Dude, You Just Got Anchored

My sales rep called me seeking help on a deal he was negotiating. His proposal for the services his client wanted was $30,000. We had been selected by the stakeholders as the VOC.

"They came back with an offer of $15,000. Roland (the buyer) said he's ready to sign the contract today at that price. I'm thinking that we should go back in at $17,000. I'm pretty sure that I can get him to sign. What do you think?"

I started laughing. "Dude, you just got anchored!" There was silence on the other end. He wasn't tracking.

Anchoring is a particularly insidious human bias in which our brains make snap decisions and subsequent judgements based on an initial piece of information. For example, if the buyer begins the negotiation with a red herring like "your competitor is 20% lower," you will tend to begin your sales negotiation at that starting point.

In this case, you've got the dual challenge of keeping yourself from being anchored at 20% and being careful not to chase the "your competitor's price" red herring. What your competitor is offering is irrelevant. You were selected as the vendor of choice. The stakeholders want to do business with you. You must also consider the source of the information. In whose best interest is it to feed you that line?

Ignore red herrings like this. Focus on your Value Bridge and on diffusing the anchor.

In sales negotiations, once an anchor is established, the negotiation tends to proceed in relation to this point—whether that point is valid and reasonable or not. It's just the way the human brain works.

Anchoring is one of you most formidable adversaries at the sales negotiation table. Dozens of studies by psychologists have demonstrated just how utterly susceptible humans are to anchoring—even when the anchors are ridiculous.

My rep was about to make a big mistake. His first move was to counter the anchor as if it (the $15,000 offer) was valid. With just one move (check), the buyer had anchored him to a number that cut our profits and his commission in half.

Thankfully I caught him just in time. I coached him to diffuse the anchor by discussing the buyer's criteria for success and explaining his position first. Then if he still needed to make a price concession, that concession should not be more than $800 and a precise number. He needed to shift the focus back to his anchor—the proposal.

My rep was unsure. He said, "Roland is never going to go for this." But he gathered up his courage and countered with a $680 reduction off his original rate. It worked. Roland came back to him with a counter of $25,000. They settled at $28,375. It was the last time he ever allowed himself to be anchored by a buyer.

Diffusing Anchors

There are many ways to diffuse anchors. Above all, you must remain alert so you can recognize when you are being anchored. Awareness is the key.

Counter Higher   In cases in which a buyer is completely unreasonable, I will counter with an offer that is higher than my original proposal. It is an extreme position, and I rarely use this tactic. But when I do it, it almost always gets their attention and snaps them out of their pattern. They want to go back to the original number—*my* anchor.

Take-Away   Rather than responding with a counter, you can take something away that is important and valuable to the stakeholders. "In order to come in at that number, we'd need to remove the onsite installation team from this and let you and your team handle the installation on your own."

Highly effective sales negotiators take away solutions that impact the future state of desired business outcomes. They remove the very solutions the stakeholder group helped develop through consensus during the sales process. These solutions are the heart of the deal and what the stakeholders have indicated are most important to them.

In other words, effective negotiators reach into the ROI equation:

ROI = (MBOs + EBOs) − Price

and change the shape of the ROI by removing solutions—removals that negatively impact the stakeholder group's desired MBOs and EBOs. Because stakeholders find it very difficult to give back the things that they said they wanted, they're compelled to stop nego-tiating and align on an agreement.

Take the Deal off the Table   When an anchor is so extreme that it's ridiculous, an easy way to diffuse it is taking the entire deal off of the table and replace it with another option.

"John, based on what you just said, I think perhaps the best thing for us to do is to step back and see if we can find a better solution that will better fit into your budget."

This is yet another form of the take-away. Either it will get their attention and make them more reasonable, or it will let them off the hook. If you really were outside of their budget, it can shift them into a more collaborative posture in which you work together on a new proposal that is a better fit.

When this tactic gets their attention, they'll argue back that they wish to stick with the original proposal. This puts you firmly in control and moves them back to your original anchor. At this point, the buyer will work with you to find a way to align on an agreement.

If they don't come back to you, there was never a deal to be had anyway.

In other situations with extreme counter anchors, it might just make sense to walk away rather than even engage in a con-versation at all. If the deal is small or far outside your IQP, there is no reason to stick around. If you have a full pipeline, deals that are advancing, and little time for games, it may be good time to pick up and go home. If the stakeholder has gone beyond being unengaged to hostility and rudeness, your best move is to find better opportunities.

Effective sales negotiators manage the damaging disruptive emotion of attachment. They are disciplined enough to walk away from prospects as soon as they feel that the probability of nego-tiating a reasonable outcome and closing a deal moves below an acceptable threshold.

Put Them in Your Shoes. Perhaps the buyer stakes out an extreme position that is nonnegotiable or deep inside your limit zone and then digs in, saying, "This is absolutely my best offer—take it or leave it."

Respond with something like, "Gosh, Beverly, I really want to work with you, but at that price we aren't even making a profit. It seems like we are at an impasse. I'm curious; if you were in my situation, what would you do?"

This tactic can work brilliantly to move the buyer off their take-it-or-leave-it position when you deliver it the right way with the right tone. Tone is everything. The wrong tone will turn this into an argument. Make sure it sounds like a sincere, honest question, without a hint of sarcasm.

How Can We Still Work Together? This is my favorite tactic for diffusing extreme anchors. It almost always works. When a buyer attempts to anchor me to an extreme position, I ask a simple question that also performs as a subtle take-away: "If I couldn't do that, how can we still work together?"

This question:

- Allows you to avoid saying no or reacting harshly
- Makes you seem sincere and collaborative
- Indicates that there may be other options
- Forces them into a position where they must re-enroll in the negotiation—a form of commitment and consistency
- Puts the ball in their court to come up with a reasonable solution
- Moves the conversation from combative to collaborative

Red Herrings

"Your competitor came in 20% less than you."

"All the other proposals I received offered free installation."

"Because your prices came in so high, we're considering taking this in-house."

"We heard that your competitor is going to be releasing a new version of their software soon. We may want to wait for that before we make a decision."

Buyers will make informational statements like this to goad you into making concessions. But they are just red herrings that cause you to lose control.

Most red herrings are part of the buyer's script. Just words to justify their position for why you should give them concessions.

Rarely are these red herrings logical. For instance, consider the statement: "Your competitor came in 20% less than you." Think about it rationally—if the competitor was that much lower:

Why in the world is this buyer still at the negotiation table?

Why haven't they already purchased from your competitor?

Why did they choose you as their vendor of choice?

It doesn't make logical sense, which is exactly why you should not chase such red herrings. If you do, you'll spend your time, energy, and emotions on the red herring rather than aligning on an agreement.

Anchor Diffusion Example

Here is an example of the right way and wrong way to diffuse an anchor or a red herring. To illustrate, I'll use a *very simple price negotiation*. I've intentionally removed the complexity so that you can see the moves.

In this scenario, the sales rep sells used capital equipment. The buyer is interested in purchasing an excavator with a list cost of $100,000.

WRONG WAY

Buyer: "I like this piece of equipment. What's the lowest price you can give me?

Seller: "I can knock $10,000 off if you are buying today."

Buyer: "Ok, thanks. I'm looking at a couple of other excavators with your competitors. Let me think about it, and I'll get back to you."

Three days later ...

Buyer: "I'm still interested in that excavator. I know you said you could take $10K off, but I think I can get a better deal from your competitor. What else can you do?"

Seller: "Well, I can come down another $7,500. How does that sound?"

Buyer: "That sounds good. Let me take that back to my partner and see what he thinks."

Two days later ...

Buyer: "Is that excavator still for sale?"

Seller: "Yes. Are you ready to buy it?"

Buyer: "Maybe. I talked it over with my partner, and he feels like with the number of hours on this piece of equipment that you need to give us a better deal."

Seller: "I've already come down almost 20%. I don't think I can go any lower."

Buyer: "Come on. You know this is only worth $75K."

Seller: "$82.5K is a great price for this machine."

Buyer: "I know you can do better. Throw me a bone."

Seller: "OK. How about we meet in the middle at $78K. Will that work?"

Buyer: "That sounds good. Let me take that back to my partner."

Seller: "OK, don't hesitate to call me with questions"

The next day …

Buyer: "Hey, I spoke to your competitor. They have the same machine and quoted me $74K. I like you better, though. If you can match that price, we're ready to go."

Seller: "OK. Give me just a second to run this by my boss."

Seller: (a few minutes later): "You've got a deal. Let's get this written up."

RIGHT WAY

Buyer: "I like this piece of equipment. What's the lowest price you can give me?"

Seller: "I'm just curious; why do you like this machine?"

Buyer: "We're looking for a Caterpillar with low hours. We have a big project coming up and need the additional equipment. We can't afford to be doing a lot of maintenance."

Seller: "I'm glad you came to us. Not only does this machine have low hours, but it has also had regular service. We have all the maintenance records. You won't find many like it on the market. It's a great buy. Why don't I send over the maintenance records, and if you feel like this machine is right for you, we can go over our out-service process and price."

Buyer: "OK, we'll take a look at it."

Later that afternoon …

Buyer: "We'd like to buy the excavator, but we need you to come down on your price. Your competitors have similar equipment listed for $20,000 lower than you do."

Seller: "The same equipment?"

Buyer: "Yes. What can you do on price so we can get this done?"

Seller: (knows that this is a bluff): "Honestly, if you are finding Cat excavators in the same condition with all the maintenance records for $20K less, my advice is to jump on it. That's a really good deal."

Buyer: "Well, uh … what can you do?"

Seller: "Are you ready to buy this machine now?

Buyer: "Yes, I want it, but I need you to help me out on the price."

Seller: "I'm open to a reasonable offer."

Buyer: "How about $87,000?"

Seller: "Ouch! I'm not going to be able to get there. How about $97,357?"

Buyer: "Can you get me to $94,000?"

Seller: "I can get to $96,523, plus we are going to out-service this machine top to bottom before we deliver it to you. That way, you know it's going to run well so you can get your project done without interruption."

Buyer (thinking): "OK, that works. What do we need to do next?"

The Flinch and Pause

One of the most common ways that master negotiators disrupt anchors and draw out more concessions without working any harder is the pained flinch and pause. When the buyer asks you to make a deep concession or tries to anchor you to a very low number, sigh, make a surprised sound, or push air between your lips while shaking your head. Then allow a few seconds of silence to sit in the air.

This may trigger the buyer to keep talking and make a more reasonable offer. Silence is powerful leverage. People tend to fill in the space when there is silence. The pause also gives you a moment to gather your thoughts and avoid being anchored. Most importantly, you clearly signal, without saying no, that you are not going there.

But beware! The flinch and pause works the other way. Any buyer who has had formal training on negotiation has learned this tactic. It's powerful, and when they use it, buyers easily pull deep concessions from salespeople with little effort other than flinching and leaving them hanging in awkward silence.

The Power of Silence

Silence is powerful, but you cannot allow it to intimidate you. Don't allow the flinch and pause to goad you into handing over your paycheck. Don't be the one to fill in the empty space.

One of the hardest parts of giving and taking is learning to shut up after you've made an offer or counteroffer. That awkward moment of silence can seem unbearable. It feels like an eternity. Because you don't know how the buyer will respond, it causes you to feel vulnerable.

In this moment of weakness, you start talking, and talking, and talking. You overexplain yourself and offer more concessions. You come off as unsure of yourself and untrustworthy. You blab on and on until you talk the buyer, who was ready to agree to your terms, into asking for even more concessions.

After you put your offer on the table, be silent. Despite the alarm bells going off in your adrenaline-soaked mind, despite your pounding heart, sweaty palms, and fear, you must bite your tongue, sit on your hands, put the phone on mute, shut up, and allow your buyer to respond. You will be surprised at how often they are ready to align on an agreement if you just demonstrate a little patience.

Take-Aways and the Scarcity Effect

If anchoring is your most formidable adversary at the sales negotiation table, then the take-away is your most powerful ally. The take-away is psychological leverage that grabs your buyer at both the subconscious and conscious levels and pulls them toward you. It causes them to act.

It is because the one thing that humans want more than anything else is *what they can't have*. This is called the *scarcity effect*. This includes anything that is exclusive, hard to get, or in limited quantities—especially if other people want it too.

It also extends to anything you take off the table. Noncomplementary behavior is a form of take-away, as is relaxed, assertive confidence. When you indicate through your demeanor that you are unattached to the outcome and are willing to walk away, it pulls the other person toward you and compels them to want to align on a deal.

Everyone wants to be pursued. It makes us feel good. When you are calm, cool, and relaxed, and when you wear the "I don't need this deal" poker face, you are taking that away from your stakeholders. This causes them to want it even more. At the subconscious level, this behavior flips the script, and they begin trying to win you back. It gives you powerful leverage that alters their behavior.

The take-away technique plays a starring role in your give-take plays. When you give a concession, you *always* take something away. This is important, because whenever you take something away from the buyer, their attention is heightened and suddenly they want it back. Once these take-aways become too valuable and painful to give back, the buyer will stop negotiating and align on an agreement.

A calm, relaxed delivery and silence are critical to making a take-away technique work. It's a nuanced technique.

After pulling something back, shut up. Be patient. Wait for it. Like a magnet, the take-away pulls the buyer toward you, flips the script, and gives you control of the situation. At a heightened level, they'll cling to or even fight for what you just took away.

In other cases, because you made what you are taking away feel so valuable and demonstrated that as a negotiator you won't just roll over, the buyer will move to a more collaborative stance— "How can we work together?" versus "What else can you give me?" The take-away earned you respect. You disrupted their aloofness, making it much easier to align on an agreement.

36

Lock It Down

General George Patton once said that you should "never pay for the same ground twice." This is sound advice in war and negotiation. The last thing you want is to believe you have an agreement only to learn (once you've counted your chickens) that you don't.

Just because you are communicating doesn't mean you are agreeing. Just because the buyer nods their head, smiles, or says the word "yes" doesn't mean you have an agreement.

Salespeople make these assumptions every single day and, in doing so, get burned. Honestly, it's heartbreaking to watch. This is why no one on my team gets to celebrate a deal until we have ink on paper, digital ink on a contract, or payment in hand.

The number one reason why salespeople end up with assumptions rather than a closed deal is that they fail to *ask*. In sales negotiations, *when you fail to ask, you fail*.

Asking is the most important discipline in sales negotiation. It's the key to locking agreements down and getting ink. You must ask for what you want—directly, confidently, and assertively.

When you believe you are aligned with the buyer on an agreement, ask immediately for a commitment and lock it down with:

1. **Payment** in the form of a credit card, check, digital payment, or wire transfer.
2. **Signed agreement or purchase order** in real or digital ink.
3. **Symbol of agreement.** When I know, trust, and have a history with people, a handshake together with explicit confirmation of a final agreement is considered a lock.
4. **Letter of understanding (LOU).** In some complex negotiations, getting a final deal is a journey rather than an event. In such cases, a letter of understanding following each meeting should be sent to confirm what you have agreed on and what you still need to negotiate.

The Discipline to Ask Is the Real Secret to Getting Ink

If you want to succeed in sales negotiations and get ink consistently, you *must* master the discipline of asking. It is the most important discipline in all phases of the sales process. Asking is the key that unlocks:

- Qualifying information
- Appointments
- Demos
- Leveling up to decision makers or down to influencers
- Information and data for building your business case
- Next steps
- Micro-commitments
- Buying commitments
- INK

In sales, asking is everything. If you fail to ask, you'll end up carrying a box of stuff from your desk to your car before going to the unemployment line. Your income will suffer. Your career will suffer. Your family will suffer. You will suffer.

When you fail to ask, you fail. It's the truth, and this truth will not change.

You Are Not Getting What You Want Because You Are Not Asking for What You Want

If you constantly find that it is a challenge to land the next appointment, get time with decision makers, get information from stakeholders, level up higher in the organization, or close the deal, it's not because you lack prospecting skills, closing skills, the right words to say, or tactics for handling sales objections and negotiation.

You are not getting what you want because you are not *asking* for what you want. Why? Because, nine times out of ten, you are insecurely and passively beating around the bush because you are afraid to hear the word *no*.

In this state, confident and assertive asking gets replaced with wishing, hoping, and wanting.

You hesitate and use weak, passive words. Your tone of voice and body language exude insecurity and desperation. You wait for your prospect to do your job for you and set the appointment, set the next step, or close the deal themselves.

But they don't.

Instead, they resist and push back. They put you off, brush you off, turn you off, and sometimes steamroll right over you. In sales negotiation, passive doesn't work. Insecurity won't play. Wishing and hoping don't make a viable strategy.

Only direct, confident, assertive asking gets ink.

There Is No Silver-Bullet

For as long as salespeople have been asking buyers to make commitments, they have been obsessed with shortcuts and silver bullets that will miraculously close the deal without the need to ask for it.

Salespeople seek techniques for closing just as golfers pursue the perfect putter. And an endless line of pseudo-experts panders to the deep insecurities of vulnerable salespeople with false and dangerous claims that their secrets give salespeople the power to close the deal every time.

They are wrong. There is no secret, and you should never take advice from these charlatans who couldn't sell their way out of a paper bag.

- There is no perfect putter that will take twenty strokes off your golf game overnight.
- There is no magic fairy dust that will take the sting out of rejection and the natural conflict of the sales negotiation table.
- There are no silver-bullet words that will stun prospects into submission.
- There are no perfect scripts that will turn *no* into *yes* every time.
- There is no easy button that will close the deal every time.

This is the brutal and undeniable truth: Everything in sales begins with and depends on the discipline to *ask*. To *succeed* at the sales negotiation table, you must ditch your wishbone, grow a backbone, and lock the deal down with INK.

37

The Next Chapter and the Race to Relevance

In the top-floor meeting room of a luxury hotel in Mumbai, India, the participants in my training session were growing restless. Through the windows behind them I could see the ocean stretching out into the blue horizon. The boats, tiny below us, were coming back from a day of fishing.

I was delivering a comprehensive Sales EQ training session to a group of Indian sales professionals. We'd been working hard for three days, trying to create a major shift in their mindset about the sales process and ways to approach the stakeholders.

They'd been eager and engaged earlier, but now that we were nearing the end of our time together, I sensed that something was brewing. We were deep into a conversation about how to gain consensus among the stakeholders on the business outcome map following the discovery stage of the sales process, when I was interrupted by a participant in the front row.

"Jeb, this all sounds good for America, but this is India. I don't think you understand what buyers are like here. We can do all the things you are teaching us, but it won't matter, because the buyers in India only care about getting a low price." Naveen's voice shook with frustration.

You Don't Understand

Jeb, you don't understand. I hear those same words every week, in every training session, wherever I am in the world.

When I'm overseas, it's "Jeb, you don't understand because you are an American." When I'm in North America, I hear, "Jeb, you don't understand because our company (or product, service, customers, buyers, niche, vertical, geographic region—pick a card, any card) is different."

I've heard it all. From Moscow to Milan, Lisbon to London, Shanghai to Sao Paulo, Dubuque to Dubai, and Atlanta to Amsterdam. There are a thousand excuses and justifications for why salespeople can't sell. Earlier this year, a rep in a Fanatical Prospecting Boot Camp even spent ten minutes attempting to convince me, with a straight face, that buyers in Virginia don't like to be called before 10 a.m.—a ridiculous explanation for why his pipeline was empty.

"Our buyers are different."

"It doesn't work like that in our industry (company, culture, country)."

"The buyers we deal with are better negotiators than in other industries."

"It doesn't matter what we say or do, our buyers only care about price."

"The buyers in our industry just commoditize us."

These are the lies and excuses that sales professionals in every corner of the globe tell themselves to justify why they get rolled at the sales negotiation table.

Just a few weeks ago in Chicago, I was delivering a Sales EQ training to a group of experienced national account managers—the salespeople responsible for interacting with my client's (a global manufacturer) largest accounts. One of the participants was absolutely adamant.

"But Jeb, you don't understand. Everything you are teaching us about advancing deals through the sales process and bridging to value might make sense at other companies, but our customers are different. They only care about price."

I smiled. It was pure delusion. "Neal, just so I understand, your products are the highest-priced in your market, right?"

"Yes," he responded, "in some cases we are much higher than our competitors."

"How come you are so much higher?" I asked.

"Because our products are of much better quality and our service is superior. We are hands down the best in the business and deliver far more value than our competitors." He said this proudly, glancing at his sales leader in the back of the room, who nodded in approval.

That's when I whacked him right dead in the forehead with the truth. "OK, Neal, I'm curious. If your prices are the highest in the market, and in *your* words, all of your customers 'only care about price,' then how is it possible that your company is still in business?"

What followed was stuttering and stammering, then finally . . . awareness.

The brutal truth is that if the only thing your customers care about is price, your company doesn't need you, because they can just list the product online and let buyers click and buy.

Back in Mumbai

My training room in Mumbai was filled with people who sold the highest-quality and highest-priced brand in their market niche. After I was interrupted, I led them through similar logic.

But not willing to accept the truth, they switched gears. "Jeb, it's not like in America. Indian buyers are the *best* negotiators in the world. Our culture here is different."

If there had been a camera on me it would have recorded my stunned expression as I stared back at a group of college-educated Indian sales professionals who were reasoning with me that they were incapable of negotiating with Indian buyers because those buyers were so tough to deal with. It was cultural, they argued, but they were missing the blinding flash of the obvious—*they* were also part of that culture.

But as I stood there shaking my head, I did have empathy for their frustration. In my early twenties, I had a job selling advertising for a local radio station. My city had a thriving Indian community, and my assigned territory was thick with Indian-owned businesses.

Just like my students in Mumbai, I found Indian business owners formidable. They were tough negotiators who beat me up badly. I was frustrated and failing miserably at winning deals in the Indian business community. I was even considering quitting my job.

One Saturday afternoon, while sitting on my parent's back porch, I grumbled about it to my dad. "They don't play fair!" I whined, hoping for a sympathetic ear. "Those Indian business owners don't understand how we do things here in America. I hate working with them!"

My dad's response was not at all what I expected. Rather than taking my side, he admonished me, his tone harsh.

"This isn't *their* problem, Jeb; it's *your* problem. Those business owners are doing exactly what they are supposed to do. They are protecting their businesses and their bank accounts. Do you think they owe you something? Are they supposed to just roll over because 'that's the way we do things in America?'"

I tried to interrupt, but he held his hand up. He wasn't finished. "Your problem is that your attitude about this is so poor that you can't see the truth. Instead of looking in the mirror at yourself, you are making excuses and blaming the very people that you want to be your customers."

"You need to get your head out of your ass and wake up. They don't need to change—*you do*. You need to become a better salesperson. You need give them a reason why they should do business with you at the prices you are asking them to pay. You are not entitled to their advertising business. You have to earn it."

I was stung by his words. My face flushed hot, and I was deeply embarrassed, because I was forced to confront my biases and piss-poor attitude. I fumed for the rest of the afternoon, angry that he had called me out so harshly.

But he was right, and I knew it. If I wanted to win deals with the Indian business owners in my territory, I had to change the only three things that I could control—my actions, reactions, and mindset. It was time to start managing my emotions, adjust my attitude, change my beliefs, walk in those doors confidently, and become a better sales professional.

And that's exactly what I did. I'm not saying it was easy, and it didn't happen overnight. It's never easy to shift your mindset like that. Over time, though, I learned the right way to approach the Indian business owners with the right questions. I learned how to keep them engaged and how to bridge to and demonstrate my value.

Most importantly, I learned how to control my emotions and stand toe-to-toe with these master negotiators. I realized that I found it so hard to negotiate with them because they controlled their emotions, and I didn't control mine.

They wanted the very best deal for their business, while I just wanted them to like and validate me. When they showed little emotion, when they didn't feed my need for significance, I felt frustrated, insecure, and dismissed. That was my problem—not theirs.

The salespeople with me in that room in Mumbai were experiencing the same disruptive emotions. My story helped them become aware of that truth, and our conversation shifted from excuses to honest and transparent discussion about how they needed to change and do things differently to win for their team.

Learning the Hard Way

After my stint in advertising, I landed a job with a bigger company selling in an insanely competitive industry.

The products and services I sold weren't sexy and were perceived to be, and treated as, commodities by most buyers. But the job was lucrative. I learned early on that sexy industries and mundane industries often have an inverse correlation to the size of commission payouts. Since I liked money, I stuck with my mundane product.

"You guys are all the same. Just give me your best price" was the regular refrain from buyers who perceived no difference between the many vendors in my niche. What made things worse was that the sales collateral and pitches from each of the players in the market, including my company, were essentially the same. It was no wonder that buyers could not see any real difference between us.

The competition was fierce and aggressive. The buyers were demanding and unforgiving, because they knew they were in the driver's seat. Every deal was a dog fight. I learned not to negotiate until I'd been selected as the vendor of choice. To do otherwise was to die a death of a thousand cuts.

In this grueling, cutthroat, winner-takes-all world, salespeople who found it difficult to differentiate beyond price burned out quickly. Those who couldn't negotiate survived on the crumbs that were left on the floor.

For salespeople who relied on a pure price play, the race to the bottom in this hyper-competitive environment was short and fast, and usually ended abruptly—the odds weren't much better than going down to the local convenience store and scratching lottery tickets.

The only way to win and win consistently was to rise above the crowd. It required me to treat each opportunity like a chess match. There was no easy button. Each deal had to be *earned*. Fortunately, I'd learned some valuable lessons from my days selling advertising to Indian business owners.

Inside this new crucible I learned how to master the sales game board and MLP strategy. I learned that emotional connections mattered, because they gave me leverage. I learned that leverage allowed me to influence buyer behaviors, flip the "just give me your best price" script, and gain control of the process.

Once I gained control of the process, step by step by step, I could shift stakeholders from their commodity lens, where every competitor looked the same and "the only thing that mattered was price," to perceiving me as their only real alternative.

The Race to Relevance

Since then, much has changed. Technology is constantly accelerating disruptive change, and business is moving infinitely faster. Lower barriers to entry have released a relentless onslaught of "me-too" competitors. Social media and the Internet have reshaped how buyers get information.

Buyers have more power, more information, and more control over the sales process than at any time in history. Along with this, they've lost all patience for kitchen-sink data dumps of features and benefits and canned product pitches.

Buyers expect more from their interactions with salespeople. Buyers want to emerge from sales conversations with value beyond a summary of the rep's marketing brochures. They are sick and tired of being treated like transactions.

Legions of salespeople are coming face-to-face with a cold, hard truth: price is not a competitive edge. Competing on price just makes you look like everyone else, and that expands the buyer's alternatives and power at the sales negotiation table.

At this very moment, two races are occurring in the sales profession—a race to the bottom and a race to relevance (see Figure 37.1).

The race to the bottom is a competition for the lowest price. In this race, even when you win, you lose. If all you have to talk about is price, if all you can do is regurgitate marketing brochures, then all your buyers will care about is price.

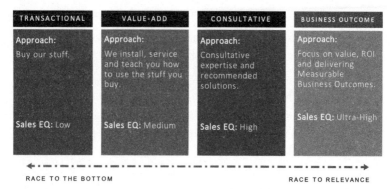

Figure 37.1   The Four Types of Sales Approaches.

The race to the bottom leads to extinction. When the only thing that matters is price, what you are selling will move to the Internet, and you cannot compete with the Internet.

In this new paradigm, though, elite groups of sales professionals are crushing it. In this age of transparency, where information is ubiquitous and buyer attention spans are fleeting, these ultra-high performers are keeping prospects engaged, creating true competitive differentiation with a focus on business outcomes, and shaping and influence buying decisions by being relevant and valuable to their stakeholders.

To win for your team, you must look beyond price and features. Instead, you must focus on human relationships, deal strategy, and have a sincere desire to help your customers. To separate yourself from competitors and become your customer's only alternative, you must demonstrate, deliver, and sustain measurable and emotional business outcomes for your customers.

The brutal truth is that products and services of all kinds can quickly become commoditized. Prices can easily be matched. *You,* however, cannot. Therefore, you must bring proven processes, business acumen, thoughtfulness, and expertise to the table. *You* must become a sustainable, ongoing, and adaptable professional resource for stakeholders by delivering true value and ROI.

Notes

Chapter Five

1. Antonio Damasio, *Descartes' Error: Emotion, Reason, and the Human Brain* (New York: Putnam, 1994; rev. ed., Penguin, 2005).
2. Google Dictionary
3. Dictionary.com
4. Vocabulary.com

Chapter Twelve

1. In 2011, Fisher and Ury published a third edition of *Getting to Yes*. The updated edition was edited by Bruce Patton and incorporates Fisher and Ury's responses to criticisms of their original 1981 book.
2. Daniel Kahneman, *Thinking, Fast and Slow* (New York: Farrar, Straus and Giroux, 2011).

Chapter Eighteen

1. https://youtu.be/Ks-_Mh1QhMc
2. https://jamesclear.com/body-language-how-to-be-confident

3. https://lifehacker.com/the-science-behind-posture-and-how-it-affects-your-brai-1463291618

Chapter Nineteen

1. https://www.nytimes.com/2014/02/23/sports/olympics/olympians-use-imagery-as-mental-training.html?_r=0
2. https://www.sportpsychologytoday.com/sport-psychology-for-coaches/the-power-of-visualization/

Chapter Twenty

1. https://www.ncbi.nlm.nih.gov/pmc/articles/PMC1447286/
2. Tara Bennett-Goleman, *Emotional Alchemy* (New York: Harmony Books, 2002).

Chapter Thirty-One

1. Belinda Luscombe, "Why We Talk About Ourselves: The Brain Likes It," *Time*, May 8, 2012, http://healthland.time.com/2012/05/08/why-we-overshare-the-brain-likes-it/.
2. Diana I. Tamir and Jason P. Mitchell, "Disclosing Information About the Self Is Intrinsically Rewarding," *Proceedings of the National Academy of Sciences* 109, no. 21 (May 22, 2012): 8038–8043, www.pnas.org/content/109/21/8038.full.

Chapter Thirty-Three

1. Robert B. Cialdini, *Influence: The Psychology of Persuasion,* (rev. ed., New York: Harper Business, 2006).

Acknowledgments

It is impossible to write a book like *Inked* on one's own:

Anthony Iannarino, thank you for letting me have the title *INKED*. We all have that one title in our back pocket that we're saving for the right book. You are a wonderful and selfless friend to let me have yours.

My deep appreciation goes out to Mike Weinberg for writing the foreword and your encouragement—just when I needed it the most. Your enthusiasm for this book means the world to me.

Mark Hunter, you rock! Your work helped inspire *INKED*, and I am deeply grateful for your friendship.

A special thank you to Patrick Tinney for writing *Unlocking Yes*. You are a huge inspiration to me.

I am so blessed to have the John Wiley & Sons team in my corner. To Shannon Vargo, Matt Holt, Peter Knox, Sally Baker, Deb Schindlar, and Vicki Adang, my deepest gratitude for your support, encouragement, and flexibility. I am very proud to be a Wiley author!

Because there is no true one-size-fits-all in sales, I spent several years observing sales negotiations in real life before writing the first word of *INKED*. This would not have been possible without the wonderful companies and people we call clients and friends who gave me access to their teams and shared their thoughts and ideas with me.

A huge thank you to my amazing team at Sales Gravy. You are making such a profound impact on the sales profession. Your dedication to advancing sales as a profession is unwavering. Thank you so very much for always having my back and making each *next* book possible.

My heartfelt gratitude to Abby Lester and Jason Eatmon for your invaluable help with editing this book.

Finally, to my beautiful wife Carrie, thank you for the sacrifices you make to give me the space to be creative. I know it is not easy living with that kind of crazy. I love you!

Training, Workshops, and Speaking

When it comes to sales training, we wrote the book—literally. Sales Gravy offers a complete system and a comprehensive suite of training programs and workshops for sales professionals, leaders, account executives, SDRs, BDRs, account managers, customer service professionals, and channel managers.

Our classroom-based training programs, instructor-led virtual training, self-directed online learning, and short workshops include:

Sales Negotiation Skills

Business Outcome Selling Strategies

Sales Objections Boot Camp

Sales EQ

Fanatical Prospecting Boot Camp

Sales Engagement Sequencing Strategies

Complex Account Prospecting Skills

Fanatical Military Recruiting

Military Recruiting EQ

Coaching Military Recruiting

Situational Coaching

Coaching Ultra-High Performance

Message Matters

Business Guidance Selling (cloud, SaaS, IoT)

Channel EQ

Enterprise Sales Skills

Customer Experience Selling (B2C)

Adaptive Account Management

Customer EQ

Adaptive Partnering (channel management)

Adaptive Mentoring

All training programs are delivered by our certified professional trainers or may be licensed and delivered by your learning and development team. We offer self-directed learning via the Sales Gravy University Platform (https://www.SalesGravy.University), instructor-led remote learning via a virtual classroom experience, and rich in-classroom learning experiences.

The training media, educational design, and delivery connect with adult learning preferences and are responsive to multigenerational learning styles. We employ an active learning methodology that blends interactive instruction with experiential learning elements and role-playing scenarios to create reference experiences that anchor key concepts and make training stick.

In addition to training, we specialize in developing custom sales onboarding learning paths for new hires and sales playbooks.

For more information, please call 1-844-447-3737, or visit https://www.SalesGravy.com.

About the Author

Jeb Blount is the author of eleven books and among the world's most respected thought leaders on sales, leadership, and customer experience.

Through his global training organization, Sales Gravy, Jeb and his team help a who's who of the world's most prestigious organizations reach peak performance *fast* by optimizing talent, leveraging training to cultivate a high-performance culture, developing leadership and coaching skills, and applying more effective organizational design.

Jeb spends more than 250 days on the road each year delivering keynote speeches and training programs to high-performing sales teams and leaders across the globe.

As a business leader, Jeb has more than 25 years of experience with Fortune 500 companies, small and midsize businesses (SMBs), and start-ups. His flagship website, SalesGravy.com, is the most visited sales-specific website on the planet.

Jeb is the author of eleven books, including:

Inked (John Wiley & Sons, 2020)
Fanatical Military Recruiting (John Wiley & Sons, 2019)
Objections (John Wiley & Sons, 2018)
Sales EQ (John Wiley & Sons, 2017)

Fanatical Prospecting (John Wiley & Sons, 2015)

People Love You: The Real Secret to Delivering a Legendary Customer Experience (John Wiley & Sons, 2013)

People Follow You: The Real Secret to What Matters Most in Leadership (John Wiley & Sons, 2011);

People Buy You: The Real Secret to What Matters Most in Business (John Wiley & Sons, 2010);

Connect with Jeb on LinkedIn, Twitter, Facebook, YouTube, and Instagram.

To schedule Jeb to speak at your next event, call 1-888-360-2249, email brooke@salesgravy.com or carrie@salesgravy.com, or visit www.jebblount.com.

You may email Jeb directly at jeb@salesgravy.com.

Index

Page numbers followed by *f* or *t* refer to figures and tables, respectively.